DATE DUE

JE 10 00			
DE 2 00			
MY 2 7 01			
JE 50 01			
DE 19 01			
MY 21 02			
AP 25 03			

DEMCO 38-296

FROM WELFARE TO WORK

FROM WELFARE TO WORK

Corporate Initiatives and Welfare Reform

Felice Davidson Perlmutter

New York   Oxford
Oxford University Press
1997

y Press

'ork

Bombay   Buenos Aires
Delhi   Florence   Hong Kong
Istanbul   Karachi   Kuala Lumpur   Madras   Madrid   Melbourne
Mexico City   Nairobi   Paris   Singapore   Taipei   Tokyo   Toronto

and associated companies in

Berlin   Ibadan

Published by Oxford University Press, Inc.,
198 Madison Avenue, New York, New York 10016

Oxford is a registered trademark of Oxford University Press

Library of Congress Cataloging-in-Publication Data
Perlmutter, Felice Davidson
    From welfare to work : corporate initiatives and welfare reform /
Felice Davidson Perlmutter.
        p.   cm.
    ISBN 0-19-511015-3 (cloth). — ISBN 0-19-511016-1 (paper)
    1. Public welfare—United States—Case studies.   2. Welfare
recipients—Employment—United States—Case studies.   I. Title.
HV95.P472   1997
361.973—dc20   96-31398
                                                                CIP

1 3 5 7 9 8 6 4 2

Printed in the United States of America
on acid-free paper

To Dan—husband, partner, colleague, friend

Shall we cling to the conception of industry as an institution primarily of private interests, which enables certain individuals to accumulate wealth, too often irrespective of the well-being, the health and the happiness of those engaged in its production? Or shall we adopt the modern viewpoint and regard industry as being a form of social service, quite as much as a revenue producing process?

John D. Rockerfeller, Jr.

Profit is the key word in moving an enterprise forward. But there is general recognition today that maximizing profit at the expense of social and human values is a losing game. The much more difficult game of balancing profit with social and human values is our present concern.

Donald MacNaughton, former chairman,
Prudential Life Insurance

CONTENTS

FOREWORD

Any company that has been in existence for more than fifty years has had ample time to test its place in the market. That is certainly true for Pennsylvania Blue Shield, the state's largest health insurer. One of our longtime corporate objectives has been to be a recognized leader in health care. But leadership carries with it a responsibility to the community.

People associate a strong social mission with Pennsylvania Blue Shield because of our product, health insurance. But our social mission is not restricted to our product alone; it extends to the community in which we live. A company does not stop at the edge of the parking lots that surround its buildings. We have a life in the greater community and achieving true success as a business takes us into that community. This philosophy helps explain how Pennsylvania Blue Shield came to embark on the journey described in this book, given the convergence of circumstances that occurred in the late 1980s.

The first circumstance was our ongoing need to secure competent workers. Every employer faces the challenge of securing an adequate and appropriately trained workforce. Access to a job-ready pool of workers is likely to be governed by the forces of demographics, social conditions, and market need.

Pennsylvania Blue Shield draws its workforce from central Pennsylvania. In an effort to analyze our future workforce needs, we undertook a study entitled "Workforce 2000." Among the report's many findings that have helped us shape our recruitment efforts is the fact that we work in an area with a relatively low unemployment rate. Because of a shortage of eligible workers, we have had to reach out beyond the traditional workforce and recruit workers who may not be ready to step into the job on day one.

To find a long-term solution to the problem of building a stable workforce, we forged a public-private partnership to develop a program that had a strong training component, assured available jobs at the end of the training component, and dedicated the necessary resources for training.

Another circumstance that gave rise to our new program was business expansion. When the opportunity arose for Pennsylvania Blue Shield to take on a significant portion of new business, we used that opportunity to explore an innovative way to increase our available pool of workers. We had some limited experience in hiring welfare recipients who had been trained by Susquehanna Education and Training Company (SETCO). Various people of vision within Pennsylvania Blue Shield and the local community were able to build on that experience in designing a program to recruit and train members of the welfare community.

Dr. Felice Perlmutter has carefully researched this innovative approach that enables welfare recipients to move from welfare to work. She chronicles the path traveled by Pennsylvania Blue Shield leaders who recognized that training future workers is a way to reinforce a sense of personal hope and social responsibility. She also details the critical involvement of other leaders in government and the community who helped the program to succeed.

From the perspective of an employer, it has always made more sense to empower individuals to become gainfully employed. Clearly, the employer gains by securing a willing and able workforce. The individual gains in discovering the fulfillment and reward of work. And the public gains when individuals move from needing assistance to becoming full participating members in society. However, merely assenting to these ideas is unlikely to bring about a positive change; that takes a significant effort.

When we undertook this endeavor, we had no knowledge that our efforts would ever be recorded in a written chronicle, and we did not embark on this project expecting any recognition. Training future employees is something we decided to invest in because we had an unmet need that required attention and the skills and abilities to address it.

Over the life of the welfare-to-work program there have been many high points. To take one brief example, at one of the graduation ceremonies held at the completion of each training cycle, one of Pennsylvania Blue Shield's senior staff was seated next to one of the graduates.

He congratulated her and noted that she must feel proud about what she had accomplished. No doubt she was proud, but she was also pragmatic about her achievement. She said she now had a way to earn enough money to take her child to Disney World.

As the national debate continues on how best to restructure the welfare system in a way that honors the dignity of the individual, this book offers insight into one possible solution. The approach described is one that can be replicated and, based on our experience, one that is worth replicating.

The poet John Donne wrote, centuries ago, "No man is an island, entire of itself; every man is a piece of the continent, a part of the main. . . ; any man's death diminishes me, because I am involved in mankind; and therefore never send to know for whom the bell tolls; it tolls for thee." The poet's words speak to the most basic motivation for understanding the welfare-to-work project: we are all connected; that which diminishes one diminishes us all, and that which benefits one benefits us all.

Samuel D. Ross, Jr.
President and CEO
Pennsylvania Blue Shield

PREFACE

In this closing decade of the twentieth century our nation is in the process of redesigning a social welfare system that has been in place for the past sixty years. Virtually every aspect of current policy is being challenged, with the temper of the times generally moving toward less government intervention and more privatization. Given the highly political nature of the debate, it is not surprising that many of the arguments reflect ideological preferences rather than demonstrated findings. In spite of this, there seems to be broad-based agreement that the paths to constructive change must include finding ways to move people from welfare to work.

This essential element not withstanding, it must be recognized that this need is only one component of the welfare picture, and many other dimensions are also involved, which in turn call for broader economic and technological changes. While this book focuses on the challenge of moving people from welfare rolls to working roles, it recognizes that this transition is only a partial solution, relevant for those groups on welfare who are in fact employable; it is not a uniform formula that can be applied to all welfare recipients.

From his detailed study of Wisconsin welfare recipients, Mark R. Rank (*Living on the Edge: The Realities of Welfare Reform in America*, New York: Columbia University Press, 1994) found that most recipients are like all Americans in respecting the work ethic; they are eager to get off welfare and anxious to ensure a better life for their children. Concerning those who are unable to enter the job market, he asks, "Specifically, what is our collective responsibility for the bottom 20 percent of our population, and what ethical obligations do we as individuals and as a society have to attempt to alleviate such economic suffering and misery?" (p. 204).

His answer is

> The mark of a noble society is . . . not in the manner in which it helps the rich, but in how it helps the poor. Not in its virtues during good times, but in its character during hard times. Not in how it protects the powerful, but in how it defends the vulnerable. These are the attributes by which a great society should be judged. (p. 204)

Clearly we do aspire to be a great society, and many people of all political persuasions are deeply concerned with finding solutions that are effective both for the individual and for society. From among the many proposals that have been put forth in the ongoing discussion of welfare reform, three critical elements appear repeatedly: (1) the role of the public sector, (2) private sector involvement, and (3) work as the solution to the problem. Although a number of simplistic approaches suggest that one or another of these elements alone can solve the welfare problem, it is in fact virtually impossible to uncouple these intertwined elements.

Those who would like to "get government off our backs" propose ending public-sector involvement in welfare entirely, thereby removing critical safety nets from those who have no other recourse. As cutting taxes assumes priority, there is less money available for social programs, and the traditional approach of providing public works programs to employ welfare recipients is no longer viewed as acceptable. The assumption is that the private sector will have jobs for people who are dropped from the welfare rolls. At the same time, however, the government's role in providing training to welfare recipients to prepare them for the workplace is being sharply challenged, making it ever more difficult to get the training necessary for obtaining work in the private sector.

However, the private sector cannot go it alone, and it is not useful to view the matter as an either-or decision. Rather, the government has an appropriate and essential role in making private sector involvement possible. Furthermore, work cannot be separated from training, and preparation for work through training or special education is a sine qua non, whether an applicant comes from the welfare rolls or from any other segment of our society.

The debate over policies and programs related to work and welfare can benefit from the findings of successful programs that deal with this problem. Such programs can help us understand the conditions that are both necessary and sufficient for achieving this difficult transition from welfare to work.

The core of this book relates the experiences of a large corporation that ventured into the world of welfare. It describes a project in which Pennsylvania Blue Shield trained, hired, and retained on its workforce a cohort of former welfare recipients and demonstrates how the public and private sectors are inextricably intertwined in such efforts. This story is important for several reasons. First, it shows what elements are needed for success in moving people from welfare rolls to working roles. Second, the program is unique because several hundred workers were involved and the long-term benefits were dramatic: welfare outlays were cut and income taxes were generated as the recipients became productive workers. Moreover, Pennsylvania Blue Shield increased its pool of workers while making a substantial contribution to its community, and our entire society benefited by the integration of a large group of people who had previously been stigmatized and unable to achieve productive and respected lives.

This book is divided into four parts. Part 1 provides background material for the Pennsylvania Blue Shield case study. Individual chapters deal with the issues of welfare reform from a historical and cross-national perspective, explore the concept of corporate social responsibility, and give examples of community-oriented corporate programs. This section sets the stage for the project by exploring the employment needs of Pennsylvania Blue Shield, the local conditions, and other variables that made its welfare-to-work program possible.

Training is the subject of Part 2. A detailed account of organizational, staff, and trainee perspectives is presented with an emphasis on what elements are necessary to ensure success. Part 3 focuses on employment, analyzing the experiences of both the organization and its new workers.

Lessons from this project, of interest to both corporate leaders and legislative leaders at the federal and state levels, are the subject of Part 4. In addition, another example of a corporate program involved with community concerns other than welfare is presented. The experiences of the various actors in the Pennsylvania Blue Shield program merit attention from all corporate, government, and individual stakeholders. The program offers both inspiration and guidance as we attempt to address one of the most important issues of our time.

ACKNOWLEDGMENTS

This book has been written with the hope that it will stimulate new thinking and new action in both the public and the private sectors. It would not have been possible without the contributions of a broad array of people who were directly and indirectly involved with diverse aspects of the program. The complexity of the problem of work and welfare, as well as corporate social responsiblity, merits a consideration by this wide range of experts.

First, and foremost, thanks are due to the women who participated in the Pennsylvania Blue Shield program and who generously shared their experience and suggestions. Without their contribution, this volume would have been just another work based on an outsider's academic observations. In respect for their privacy, their names are not cited.

Of equal importance is the generous cooperation of Pennsylvania Blue Shield. Its leaders responded immediately to the author's suggestion that their welfare-to-work experience was an important story to be shared, one which could, and hopefully would, stimulate other corporations to create jobs for welfare recipients. In addition to making materials, data, and documents available, the following individuals lent their insights and expertise to this research.

My initial contact at Pennsylvania Blue Shield was Thomas Sommers, Senior Vice President for Administration, whom I met after his talk for the School of Social Administration at Temple University in November 1993. He made possible all of the follow-up contacts with the organization.

Dr. David Rippey, Director of Training and Development, paved the way for the interviews and the gathering of materials. His insights and provocative questions were important in shaping this work. Gerry Rickards, Director of Keystone Training Services, was endlessly available to share the details of the training venture, having had the most direct involvement in the program throughout its life cycle.

Senior managers at Pennsylvania blue Shield were receptive and generous with their time. Special thanks are due to Samuel D. Ross, Jr., President and CEO, George F. Grode, Senior Vice President for Corporate Affairs and Assistant to the President; and Everett Bryant, Senior Vice President for Government and Corporate Business. George Grode contributed in many ways as he shared his experience in the public sector, contacted key participants in the training program, and meticulously read the manuscript.

Donna Cheatham, Continuing Education Director at Blue Shield, Keystone trainers Stephen Noss and Marge Janos, and supervisors and middle managers Ralph Breindel, Kim Deiter, Dorothy Early, Helen Hoover, Judy Krafsig-Kearny, Harlon Robinson, Scott Tackack, Debra Stoner, and Sonya Woodward also deserve my thanks. Betty Johnson, the job counselor, was also very helpful.

Willam Roberts of Creative Training Concepts and Jim McDonald of SETCO, from the collaborating organizations, were also key informants. Pete Krauss, formerly special consultant on economic development and advisor to the Mayor of Harrisburg, provided historical background.

The Pennsylvania Department of Public Welfare, both at the state and county levels, was responsive to this project. Thanks are due at the state level to Yvette Jackson, former Deputy Secretary for Public Welfare; Dr. Sherri Heller, Deputy Secretary for Public Welfare; David Florey, Director of Research, and Janet Grier, Supervisor, both of the Bureau of Education and Training; and Craig Ford, Director of Program Employment. At the Philadelphia county office, interviews were held with Don Jose Stovall, Executive Director; William Stroup, Associate Executive Director; and Jeff Blumberg and George Reno of the Employment Unit.

Other key informants included Allan Williamson, Deputy Secretary for Employment Security, Pennsylvania Department of Labor and Industry; Charles F. Pizzi, President of the Greater Philadelphia Chamber of Commerce; Philip Price, Jr., Executive Director of the Philadelphia Plan; Nelson G. Harris, former CEO, Tasty Baking Company; Barbara Cascarello, Campus Boulevard Corporation; and Pat Irving and Joe Farrell of the Philadelphia office of the Pennsylvania Industry Council. Professor Seymour Rosenthal, Director of the Center for Social Policy,

Temple University, shared insights from his extensive experience with training and employment programs for welfare recipients.

Helene Scherer, Director for Career Services, Jewish Employment and Vocational Service of Philadelphia and Elizabeth Werthan, Legislative Assistant to Congressman Chaka Fatah, provided critical information regarding the 1996 federal and state legislation.

The quotations in the frontpiece are from Tad Tuleja, *Beyond the Bottom Line* (New York: Facts on File, 1985), p. 93, and Moses L. Pava and Joshua Krausz, *Corporate Responsibility and Financial Performance* (Westport, CT: Quorum Books, 1995), p. 6.

Research for this book was supported by a Research Incentive Fund grant from Temple University.

Special appreciation goes to my husband, Dan, and my daughter, Tova, for provided stimulating challenges, wise commentary, and excellent editorial assistance.

The descriptions, analysis, and interpretations are the sole responsibility of the author.

FROM WELFARE TO WORK

I

BACKGROUND

1

From Welfare to Work

Our nation is currently in the midst of one of the great debates of the century: how to redesign our social welfare system. In these closing years of the twentieth century a fundamental transformation has taken place which has radically revamped the welfare system as we have known it for the past sixty years. Every aspect of welfare policy has been challenged, and the challenges reflect ideological preferences more than demonstrated findings. Given the temper of the times, with the swing toward less government intervention and more privatization, the debate is likely to continue for many years; it would benefit from less heat and more light on the conditions that are both necessary and sufficient for achieving the goal of moving people from welfare to work.

There are three critical elements in the ongoing discussion of welfare reform, which is the subject of this book and the focus of this chapter. The first element is the role of the public sector, at both the federal and state levels; the second is the emphasis on work as the solution to the problem, with the locus of activity in the private sector; and the third is the stigma associated with being on welfare.

Curiously, there are several omissions in the current discussion and debate. First, there is little consideration of the historical and traditional approach of providing public works programs to employ welfare recipients. Instead, the assumption appears to be that sufficient jobs will be available in the private sector for all people who are dropped from the welfare rolls. At the same time, the role of government in providing training to prepare welfare recipients for the workplace, with both technical skills and social supports, has been sharply limited and compromised. Because many welfare recipients have no work experience, the consequence of this new approach for them will be inadequate preparation for private sector jobs.

These elements are interrelated and it is misguided to focus on any one by itself. First, the private sector cannot go it alone; government at both the federal and state levels has an appropriate, if delimited, role in stimulating and making possible private sector involvement. Second, work cannot be separated from training; preparation for work through training or education is essential whether an applicant comes from the welfare rolls or from any other segment of society. Finally, the training must provide adequate preparation for the realistic expectations of the workplace.

This book tells the story of a unique and important corporate venture into the world of welfare. The outcomes of this venture are especially important in relation to the three issues discussed above. The experience of Pennslvania Blue Shield in public welfare demonstrates the important relationship between the public and the private sectors, as well as that between training and employment in the context of work realities and welfare stigma. It also shows the importance of providing supports to welfare recipients to help destigmatize their status.

Work and Welfare: The New Reality

Almost everyone has an opinion about welfare and it is rarely a neutral one. As a consequence, the issue of welfare reform usually comes to the fore in the context of national elections, when it is used as a political pawn; candidates promise a quick fix and short-term savings in order to get votes. "Work" becomes a slogan, a promised panacea, a magic formula to be pulled from the candidate's bag of tricks.

This development should not come as a surprise given the prominance of the work ethic in our society. Made popular in the repeatedly told success stories of Horatio Alger, this ethic underpins the current approach to welfare reform. It should be noted, however, that the importance of succeeding at work through one's own efforts was first stressed when our nation was a young and dynamically growing country in need of a large workforce to help its development. Opportunities then appeared to be endless. A laissez faire government, one which governs best by governing least, was certainly compatible with the belief that every person could and should be a self-starter. Meeting the personal needs of those who failed this test was not viewed as a public responsibility, but as one reserved for local charities, usually under religious auspice.

The social and economic realities in our nation have changed strikingly since the work ethic first informed our behavior. We have become a society increasingly served by computerized technology. As a result, the need for an extensive workforce has largely disappeared; many jobs have been eliminated or converted to temporary or part-time positions. This trend has affected those in the unskilled workforce (e.g., elevator operators) as well as in the blue-collar and white-collar workforce (e.g., factory workers, secretarial staff).

It is within this context that the sharp changes in welfare policy have taken place. The new federal welfare legislation, the Personal Responsibility and Work Opportunity Reconciliation Act of 1996 (P.L. No. 104–193), has several central provisions directly related to the discussion in this book. First and foremost, in regard to the role of the public sector, the law shifts the source of power and authority from the federal government to the states, from federal entitlements to state initiatives, and from strong federal guidelines to virtually none. This is accomplished through the bill that converts Aid to Families with Dependent Children (AFDC) into a block grant called the Temporary Assistance for Needy Families (TANF), with discretion at the state level for the management of this money. The net effect of this approach has been strongly criticized, as is evident in the words of B. Hangley, Jr. ("Welfare Devolution in Greater Philadelphia," The 21th Century League, Philadelphia, PA, October 1996):

> To call the result welfare reform is something of a misnomer. Better to call it welfare devolution, because, rather than reconstruct or reform the major federal programs, Washington has eliminated them. (p. 3)

The second issue addressed in the new legislation is the primary emphasis on work, with only minimal attention paid to training. This is happening at a time when corporate America is downsizing, when white-collar and blue-collar workers, as well as professionals, are losing their jobs. The consequence is a great competition for existing jobs, a fact of life sadly experienced by all people seeking work. Displaced workers are competing with university graduates seeking to enter the workforce for the first time. Can welfare recipients be expected to compete with both of these more highly skilled and educated populations?

Some major structural problems arising from the legislation are already apparent. First, the funding is fixed, based on the highest of a state's fiscal year (FY) 1994 or 1995 spending or the average of its spending for the three years from FY 1992 to FY 1994. The funding does not reflect an increased cost of living or an increased target population at risk. Second, the money will now be given to the states in the form of a block grant with no federal requirements in relation to childcare, training, or other support services. The law limits training and education to a one-year maximum, and according to the Congressional Budget Office, there is a shortfall of 12 billion dollars in training funds (Hangley, 1996).

The withdrawal of the safety net as a result of the federal legislation puts many people at risk. A study by the Center on Budget and Policy Priorities found that as a result of government benefits, including food stamps, earned-income tax credits, and housing assistance, the number of poor dropped to 30.3 million in 1995 as opposed to the 57.6 million who would have been poor without these benefits. And children and the elderly are major beneficiaries of these programs.

Furthermore, each state will individually determine how the money will be spent and which services will be provided: a state could elect to shift a portion of its existing Social Services Block Grant funds from poor children to other populations when it transfers funds from TANF to the block grant, thus shifting benefits from welfare populations to others. Moreover, every family is limited to a five-year lifetime period of assistance; this includes all services funded under TANF (e.g., parenting classes, counseling, and emergency assistance).

The new shift of all responsibility to the states is predicated on the assumption that state governments can be more appropriately responsible and responsive to meet the specific conditions of their respective localities. An argument in support of block grants is that, in contrast to the federal programs' capitation rates where the money follows the individual client, block grants provide flexibility because the various state agencies receive them in a lump sum. Consequently, the Department of Public Welfare, for example, could spend less money on those welfare recipients who are job ready, and allocate proportionately more of the remaining funds in the block grant for the more problematic populations.

While there is much to commend the argument as it relates to proximity, one cannot ignore some fundamental problems in relation to past experience with social policy at the state level. There is great unevenness in the array of social policies among the states in response to human needs; consequently there is little assurance that being close to the situation assures an appropriate or adequate response. Furthermore, given the stigma associated with welfare, when welfare recipients are competing with unemployed and dislocated workers preference is likely to be given to retraining and reemploying former workers.

Finally, as states experience more pressure to meet increasing costs for a variety of other programs (ranging from road repair to education to environmental protection), there is no guarantee that an adequate amount of money will be protected or allocated for welfare. Welfare recipients will not be a priority population to be served when there are no strings attached to the federal dollars received in block grants.

It is essential to emphasize that state programs are not yet firmly fixed and are in flux throughout the nation. But pressure has been put on the states to develop welfare plans by July 1, 1997 in order to receive their block grants. The lessons gleaned from the Pennsylvania Blue Shield experience could be all the more instructive for states as they develop policies dealing with work and welfare.

Questions about how to design an approach to work and welfare are not new and have, in fact, been at the heart of policy debates as far back as the 1601 Elizabethan Poor Law. The problem is complex; it touches the very foundations of society because it deals not only with people's well-being on a personal level but also with economic and societal well-being. On an individual level, work gives people a feeling of worth. On a societal level, work not only integrates people into the community but, through the income tax structure, contributes to the fiscal health of the nation. If the goal is to create a group of contributing members of society, integrated through the central mechanism of work, the work available must provide adequate income and benefits for maintaining a decent lifestyle.

Fixing Welfare Policy: Training and Work

We are not alone in struggling to more effectively address the problem of welfare. Many nations in western Europe are also attempting to find appropriate and realistic solutions for large numbers of people who have experienced long-term unemployment and are supported by the welfare system, but their approach to the problem is significantly different.

In contrast to the nineteenth-century United States, the European countries whose economies were not expanding at that time began to provide an array of social welfare measures that gave their citizens a floor of security. Over time these measures came to include child or family allowances, housing supports, health care, pensions, and higher education, among others.

Today, however, in spite of a safety net available to those who are not employed, the problems associated with poverty and welfare are experienced throughout Europe. This fact prompted the Joseph Rowntree Foundation in England to challenge conventional approaches to welfare. In 1995 the Foundation report concluded, "too much public spending is directed at paying the costs of failure rather than promoting future success. Public spending appears to have got into a trap, where short-term savings have had long-term costs, in turn creating pressure for later short-term savings, in a continuing spiral" (p. 3).

In contrast to the United States, training remains the centerpiece in programs in Great Britain and western Europe, predicated on the assumption that training is necessary preparation for employment. As part of a four-part series on these programs, the *International Herald Tribune* reported that:

> After years of failing to create enough jobs, Western Europe's governments are desperately reaching out for new ways to get millions of long-term unemployed off the dole and end the mounting toll of budget and social problems. . . .

> What unites the successful programs are individual counseling and a greater emphasis on active job placement and training than traditional government programs have tended to offer. The programs are often more expensive in the short-run, but pay for themselves long-term by reducing dependency. (March 30, 1995, p. 13)

A wide range of experimental programs in Germany, Great Britain, Austria, Slovakia, Spain, France, and Holland are preparing people for work. In Austria, for example, the government's role is all pervasive and includes a variety of approaches. The Ministry of Labor and Social Affairs operates on the assumption that people must not only be given skills training, but they may also have psychological problems that must be addressed. The programs are expensive, but in the words of the *Herald Tribune* writer, "they pay for themselves in increased tax and social security revenue and savings on unpaid unemployment benefits within ten months of a participant's getting a job" (April 3, 1995, p. 15). In addition to training, these programs provide counseling and put people to work in public and nonprofit organizations.

In Great Britain many private organizations are financed by the government to provide training to help the long-term unemployed enter the job market. Recognizing that short-term training is not enough, and that the problem cannot be solved quickly, various programs offering an array of personal support services have been set up in diverse communities. The Rowntree Foundation has called for the provision of child care facilities and flextime in the workplace.

In Glasgow, a city with a high unemployment rate of 15 percent (compared to the Scottish national average of 9 percent), the training program for long-term unemployed young men, many without a high school diploma, includes eight weeks of training followed by ten months of actual employment experience in community work. "We pay them 2.8 million pounds and in return get more than 2.5 million worth of work that we would have to pay someone else for. On top of that, we get training for several hundred people" (*International Herald Tribune*, April 1–2, 1995, p. 13). Furthermore, this training serves as a springboard for getting a job by giving trainees a way to answer the question "when were you last employed?"

The recognition of the importance of training in preparation for work, so evident in Europe, was historically part of the American approach as well. The Civilian Conservation Corps of 1933, which dealt with unemployment in the Great Depression, included training in its program. The Economic Opportunity Act of 1963, the major relevant legislation of President Johnson's War on Poverty, provided training as well as work experience.

Training was raised to a new level of primacy in the 1980s by two major pieces of federal legislation under the Republican administrations of Nixon and Reagan. The Job Training Partnership Act of 1982 clearly focused on training as the strategy of choice for reducing welfare dependency, while the 1988 Family Support Act reversed the emphasis of welfare policy from income maintenance with a job training component to job training with an income maintenance component. This law was based on the view that children's well-being depends not only on having their social and material needs met but also on being in a family that is economically self-sufficient.

Training was built into many other federal programs as well. However, due to the fact that there were 154 different funding streams deal-

ing with training handled by fourteen different government agencies dif-
fused its potential impact. Much of this money was unused because many
providers of training did not know of its existence. The General High-
ways Administration, for example, had earmarked funds to be used for
training and other supportive services to help women and minorities gain
access to jobs in the highway construction industry. This was not widely
known and, as a consequence, only $800,000 of the allocated ten
million dollars was utilized in 1992 (L.L. Butler. Testimony Before
the Senate Labor and Human Resources Committee. Philadelphia:
Tradeswomen of Purpose/Women in Non-Traditional Work, 1994). The
Kassebaum-Kennedy bill was designed to address the problem and
streamline the process; unfortunately the bill died in committee.

As a result of TANF, the 1996 welfare reform legislation, training is no
longer on the federal agenda and the states have the authority, but not the
mandated responsiblity, not only to provide training but also to determine
its type and extent. Furthermore, TANF's requirements regarding work
and work-related programs demonstrate that a quick job preparation and
placement strategy has replaced a workforce investment strategy.

In our eagerness to arrive at a quick fix, there is little interest in the
lessons from the past. Clearly sixty years of experience should not be
ignored, especially when much of the experience is directly related to
the new strategies and solutions. Among the specific policies and programs that merit review, most had their origin at the federal level. The
federal government played a critical role in many ways as it conducted
work and welfare programs and as it provided money to stimulate the
states as well as the private sector to become involved in welfare. The
lack of public dollars to support services for recipients and the lack of
jobs in the private sector are major inhibitors in the process.

Even as late as 1989, but before the sharp budget cutbacks of recent
years, a study by the Congressional Budget Office showed that with the
funds then appropriated for training, only 50,000 families could be
served nationally. If each contact were successful, this number would
have only reduced welfare dependency by 1.3 percent. In today's economy, with large numbers of persons unemployed and underemployed,
it is much harder to place welfare recipients into work than it was in
1989 and the public investment must be greater.

Decentralization and block grants may indeed be effective as a partial solution but many more strategies and supports must be provided
from both the federal and state levels in today's national and interna-

tional economies. As welfare moves into the general agenda and is part of the collaboration among many state agencies, a commitment to the welfare population and a stake in its well-being must be assured, or many of the nation's poor will be lost in the shuffle.

Involving the Private Sector

A major initiative that sought to involve the private sector in training and creating work opportunities in the welfare arena was contained in federal legislation passed in 1978 which refined and expanded the Comprehensive Employment and Training Act of 1973 (CETA). The Private Sector Initiative Program provided support for the establishment of local Private Industry Councils (known as PICs). This structure allowed businesses to exert influence on training and employment efforts that targeted the unemployed poor. While there have been no formal evaluations of PIC activities, it is clear that this initiative represented a major departure in federal programming, one that for the first time sought to enlist the private sector into becoming directly involved with the employment needs of the poor.

This private sector initiative was reinforced by the the Job Training Parnership Act (JTPA) which replaced CETA in 1982 and further redefined the federal government's role in job training. More responsibility, visibility, and control were given to the private sector by this bill, which was co-sponsored by the unlikely duo of Senators Daniel Quayle and Edward Kennedy. The legislation redirected training away from the public sector and thereby reduced and simplified the role of the federal government. Training money was filtered to the private sector through local Service Delivery Areas and PICs, 51 percent of whose members were local business leaders who were given the central role in planning and developing employment training programs. The balance of members who worked with the representatives from the business community on PICs came from education, labor, and the general community.

In a second major initiative directed toward the private sector, tax credit programs at both the federal and state levels were developed to serve as an incentive for employers to provide jobs for welfare recipients. At the federal level the Targeted Jobs Tax Credit (TJTC), part of the 1977 CETA act, was intended to serve as an economic stimulus program for the creation of new jobs. With the same objective at the state level, the Employment Incentive Payment Program in Pennsylvania provided credits for up to three consecutive years and was designed to encourage employers to hire recipients of General Assistance or AFDC. The TJTC expired on January 1, 1995.

In October 1996 the Work Opportunities Tax Credit (WOTC) was enacted for a one-year period to October 1997. One of its explicitly stated goals was to target more people moving from welfare to work. However the tax credit earned by qualified employers was reduced from 40 percent under TJTC to 35 percent; and the number of hours an employer had to employ the new worker was extended from 120 under TJTC to 400 in order to assure retention of this new workforce. (It remains to be seen whether the time period will be extended since a one-year period is inadequate, especially at a time when states are not required to submit their plans until July 1, 1997).

While both the federal and state tax programs provided incentives to private employers to consider hiring welfare recipients, they did not meet the needs of small or middle-sized businesses, the fastest growing segment in the business sector. In Pennsylvania the new tax credit proposals acknowleged the needs of small and middle-sized business by providing the employer with a $1000 credit against the state business taxes for each qualifying new job created; however, employers were required to have an increase of either 25 employees or 20 percent over their current workforce in order to benefit from the tax credits.

The involvement of the private sector in dealing with welfare concerns remains a critical challenge. All strategies that can serve as inducements to corporate America should be tried, including training and tax supports at both the federal and state levels.

The Issue of Creaming

An issue frequently raised is whether only the most qualified welfare recipients should be considered for work in these programs, thereby excluding the rest of the welfare group. When such selective acceptance is viewed as negative in discussions of work and welfare, it is sometimes called "creaming." The argument against creaming applies a special standard to welfare recipients that is not ordinarily found in most educational and employment situations, where selective criteria *are* applied. When prestigious universities select new students from a large applicant pool or employers select employees from a broad group of applicants, creaming is taken for granted. It is accepted in the larger society that institutions will seek and select participants who are most likely to succeed in their settings.

In the welfare system the ability to match the individual with the appropriate training and employment opportunities is just as important if we are to maximize the probability of success. It is not unreasonable to begin with criteria that will ensure success from the individual recipient's perspective as well as from the potential employer's.

An editorial in the *New York Times* (January 21, 1994) commended the work of a private corporation, America Works, in its success with placing welfare recipients in permanent jobs. The editorial's viewpoint was that "even if America Works were only to take care of the advantaged poor, it would free the city to target its other efforts to those left behind." This approach would allow the limited welfare funds to be used to develop other approaches in working with the more disadvantaged portions of the welfare population, a strategy currently being used in the special project of the Pennsylvania Department of Welfare. Creaming is a creative and realistic approach to the complex realities in the welfare system and merits serious attention.

Common Stereotypes

Many people have strong negative opinions about welfare recipients. These myths and biases distort the nation's ability to seek appropriate solutions to help welfare recipients move into the mainstream of society. Before discussing approaches and strategies for welfare reform, it is important to understand the group of people under consideration. While it may be surprising, the following information from Congressional and other sources, compiled by the National Association of Social Workers in January 1995, and from the Department of Health and Human Services, Administration for Children and Families, can inform our proposals:

- More than two thirds of the 14 million recipients of AFDC are children.
- Families receiving AFDC do not have more children than families who are not on welfare. In 1991, more than 70 percent of all AFDC

families had two or fewer children, more than 40 percent had one child, and just 10 percent had four or more.

- Families receiving AFDC are about as likely to be white as black. In 1993, 39 percent were white, 37 percent were black, and 18 percent were Hispanic.
- AFDC benefits have fallen in value. When adjusted for inflation between 1971 and 1992 there was a 45 percent decrease in value.
- Even when combined with food stamps, benefits are below the poverty level ($11,521 per year for a family of three) in every state and below 75% of the poverty level in almost four fifths of the states.
- 63 percent of poor, female-headed families do not receive any form of public assistance benefits.
- The vast majority (70 percent) of all people entering the welfare system leave within two years and 50 percent leave within one year. Only 15 percent of all AFDC clients receive benefits for more than five years over the course of their lives.
- At least 50 percent of people who become independent of the welfare system are forced to return—often after jobs or child care fall through—but these returns are caused by external events and welfare is not a "way of life" for most recipients.

The last two of these items make it clear that any attempt to address work and welfare cannot merely focus on the characteristics and needs of the welfare population in isolation. It is necessary to simultaneously consider the characteristics of the job market and the support services that will make possible successful entry into the workforce on a permanent basis.

The federal Family Support Act, no longer in effect, mandated a range of services directly related to preparation for the world of work. These supports included education, jobs skills training, readiness activities, and two other job-oriented functions to be chosen from a menu that included job search, work experience, and on-the-job training. In addition to these activities, which were directly related to the work situation, other supports related to personal needs were also provided. The Family Support Act assured one year of transitional child care and medical benefits, two areas of primary concern to welfare recipients. The Act also provided transportation for recipients who otherwise could not get to work due to lack of public transportation. Furthermore, the federal government in-

cluded eye care and clothing allowances essential to the work requirements, although the payments were minimal and insufficient to cover
the actual costs.

All of these various supports have been found to be necessary for new
workers to succeed during the transition period between leaving welfare
and entering the workforce. It is unclear how these needs will be met
now that they are no longer mandated and are discretionary at the state
level.

Lessons from Past Programs

Extensive research has been conducted on the effectiveness of various
state models developed under the federally sponsored legislation. Conducted in thirteen states, these experimental demonstration programs
used different approaches to work and welfare. Evaluations of thirteen
diverse employment training programs for welfare recipients were conducted in 1991 by Judith Gueron and Edward Pauly. While there were
fundamental differences among the specific programs, the overall findings are important in showing clearcut benefits in the demonstrations
that were attempted at the state level under the federal legislation and
funding.

Of greatest economic interest are the first three findings:

- Almost all the programs led to earnings gains. This was true of both
  low- and higher-cost programs and services.
- Earnings were sustained for at least three years after program en-
  rollment.
- Public investments in a range of the programs were more than returned in increased taxes and reductions in welfare payments.

Lessons derived for the strategic planning of future programs are evident in the following findings:

- There was a distinction among the groups in the caseload as they
  entered the workforce. The most consistent and largest *earnings
  gains* were made by the moderately disadvantaged. The largest *welfare savings* were achieved for the more disadvantaged.
- Different services and program models have different payoffs for
  particular groups within the welfare population. Targeting resources

to the specific subgroups where they are likely to count the most is central to planning for work.

- There may be trade-offs in meeting program goals—notably in either reducing welfare expenditures or maximizing the earnings of the people in the welfare-to-work programs. A choice must be made regarding priorities.
- Understanding both the magnitude of the possible effects of the welfare-to-work programs and how such effects are achieved is essential to resource allocation decisions.
- The programs were able to serve a major portion of the welfare caseload. Thus in nine programs with a broad-targeted group, between 38 percent and 65 percent participated in at least one supplementary activity that was preparatory for taking a job.

The findings highlight the importance of federal legislation in stimulating states to design and develop programs that encourage the transition from welfare to work, and emphasize the fact that choices must be made in setting the major objectives of the programs. The specific benefits will depend on the relative importance placed on whether the program should produce more substantial earnings for welfare recipients, whether the program should maximize welfare savings, or whether the program should seek to reduce long-term dependency.

Where past welfare policies appear to have had little impact, the fault is not in the policies but in their implementation. There has been too little money, too little investment, in assuring that all eligible candidates could benefit from the various federal and state programs designed to move welfare recipients into the world of work. In transforming the welfare system it is essential that we not throw the baby out with the bathwater, that in the haste to decentralize and cut taxes, we do not ignore the findings that demonstrate that it is possible to move from welfare to work, provided that an array of needs are met.

Conclusion

The central question to be addressed is: What problems must be solved in order to create the kind of society that we want? Is the goal primarily to cut welfare expenditures so that our taxes will be lower, or is it primarily to create opportunities for individuals to lead productive and satisfying lives? Will the broader societal good be served if large groups in our population are marginalized? Or is the objective a combination of these goals, which maximize meeting the needs of individuals as well as those of society as a whole?

There is no question that in order to achieve the last objective, the public sector must remain involved, a conclusion supported by the Pennsylvania Blue Shield experience. The collaboration between the public and the private sectors is an optimal relationship made possible by public policies that underwrite the various strategies to be pursued.

This support is best assured by policies that begin at the federal level and are supported by further state legislation. Money for training, flexible personal supports for welfare recipients, and various tax incentives made possible through federal and state legislation provide the grease that lubricates the wheels to move people from welfare to work.

The complexities of work and welfare cannot be adequately addressed by partial solutions that focus only on lower taxes and a lesser role for government. These are not simple issues, nor are they unique to our society. Furthermore, there is little evidence that any one approach will remedy the problem. A serious commitment by a broad array of stakeholders is necessary to develop proposals and strategies for long-range as well as short-range solutions in shaping a society that serves both the individual and the commonweal.

The experience of Pennsylvania Blue Shield is of great importance for two reasons. First, it describes the successful foray of a major corporation into the welfare arena. Second, it addresses the social policy issues that are necessary to encourage the private sector to enter an unfamiliar and untested arena.

2

Doing Good While Doing Well

"Entrepreneurs Are Finding Rewarding Remedies for Social Ills."

Most people who start a business are driven by capitalist urges. Steve Mariotti was inspired by a vicious mugging. Instead of seeking revenge, the import–export businessman and former Ford executive decided to teach kids like his teenage assailants a real lesson: the principles of business. (*U.S. News and World Report*, October 31, 1994, p. 103)

Steve Mariotti is one of a growing number of entrepreneurs who has become directly involved with the complex and critical societal problems that plague our country. These problems affect all of us. They range from increased alienation of large segments of our society to increased violence, muggings, and weapons assaults.

Given the recognition that social problems create a formidable challenge, one that demands the creative response of many segments of our society, the question arises, does corporate America bear a responsibility for alleviating these social problems? Since the major purpose of a corporation is making profits for its shareholders, can it also make social responsiblity a part of its mission? Usually a tension exists between these two goals.

The popular, traditionally accepted viewpoint has been most clearly articulated by Milton Friedman and is aptly expressed in the title of an article he wrote for the *New York Times Magazine* (September 13, 1970): "A Friedman Doctrine—The Social Responsibility of Business Is to Increase Its Profits." But Friedman's views are being questioned as many sectors and stakeholders in our society seek new answers to dealing with the accelerating social problems of our country.

Even in the early part of the twentieth century business leader John
D. Rockefeller Jr. asked*:

> Shall we cling to the conception of industry as an institution primar-
> ily of private interests, which enables certain individuals to accumu-
> late wealth, too often irrespective of the well-being, the health and the
> happiness of those engaged in its production? Or shall we adopt the
> modern viewpoint and regard industry as being a form of social ser-
> vice, quite as much as a revenue producing process? (p. 6)

President Reagan, in the 1980s, also called on the business sector to
meet those social challenges with which government could not and
should not be involved.

Corporate social responsibility is a concept that has gained credence
with many entrepreneurs, businesses, and schools of business in recent
years, but it remains a minority viewpoint in our society. Corporate social responsibility can take many forms; the challenge is for businesses
to address societal problems that are related to the company's mission
and expertise and that they can realistically affect.

This book addresses a particular societal problem, welfare, an area
suited to corporate concern given the growing disaffection with large
government and the increasing support of privatization in our society.
Corporate America has the potential to provide jobs for welfare recipients, a potential that is of increasing importance as public employment
and public works programs are no longer available as a mechanism for
moving people from welfare to work.

A central aim of this book is to stimulate corporations and small businesses in the private sector that are ready to become involved in this
critical social issue by presenting an example of a successful program
at a large corporation. Pennsylvania Blue Shield successfully trained and
employed several hundred welfare recipients The example is instructive because it highlights the central elements in the program that underpinned its success. The discussion may also serve to stimulate social
action by firms that have not yet embraced the notion of corporate social responsibility.

This chapter discusses corporate social responsibility, in concrete
terms as it presents several examples of firms that have become involved

---

*From M.L. Pava and J. Krausz *Corporate Responsibility and Financial Performance.*
Westport, CT: Quorum Books, 1995.

in this arena. It also sets the stage for the detailed case study that follows. There is increasing awareness of and concern with community
problems in the corporate world. This case study offers one possible
model, as well as inspiration, for those who want to be a force in solving those problems.

What Is Corporate Social Responsibility?

In defining corporate social responsiblity, Moses Pava and Joshua
Krausz, in their book *Corporate Responsibility and Financial Performance* (Westport, CT: Quorum Books, 1995), state that "the core belief
is that the corporation incurs responsibilities to society beyond profit
maximization" (p. 1). While this statement captures the essence of the
idea, corporate responsibility has other dimensions as well. A discussion of corporate responsibility often includes a discussion of business
ethics and employee relations, that is, how the corporation deals with
its publics, its consumers, and its employees.

In this book the focus is even broader, addressing the role and responsibility of corporate America in the community at the local, state,
national, and international levels. All businesses are directly affected by
the world in which they operate; their ultimate well-being is affected by
their community's well-being. If social problems are severe enough in
a particular setting, the corporation will find that it cannot function.
Specifically, is there a workforce available? Are there customers for the
products? Is the community a safe place to live and work?

Corporate social responsibility is not a new concept that emerged in
the 1960s. Rather, the idea developed in the twentieth century as major
corporate entities began to emerge. Rockefeller's formulation of industry as a social service, quoted earlier, is certainly unique, but it highlights the need for a balance between financial gain and social responsibility. Rockefeller reflected a particular point in time, a particular point
of view, and a particular developmental stage in corporate life in the
United States. Not only were corporations accumulating great wealth in
the early twentieth century, but to counter negative community response
to corporate behavior they devised approaches that would improve their
image in the community. Carnegie, Ford, and Rockefeller established
foundations that focused on social concerns and perpetuated the family
name. These initaitves were readily accomplished because each business was unilaterally governed by its founding member.

In the 1950s, after World War II, there was a change in attitude regarding the role of corporate America. A book by Howard R. Bowen, *Social Responsibilities of the Businessman* (New York: Harper & Brothers, 1953), called on industry to focus on challenges other than economic ones; but it was not until the 1970s and 1980s that interest in the subject became widespread. During the 1980s many books and articles were written about the subject with titles such as "Corporate Power and Public Issues," "Corporate Responsibility: Reconciling Economic and Social Goals," "Incorporating Corporate Social Policy into Strategic Management," "Has Social Responsibility Cleaned Up the Corporate Image?", and "Sowing New Seeds for Corporate Responsibility." One article highlighted the fact that President Reagan called upon private industry not only to help the disadvantaged but also to aid cultural institutions.

These various discussions were not reserved for academics and policy experts alone. They appeared in mainstream journals serving the business community, such as *Academy of Management Review*, *Business and Society Review*, *California Management Review*, *Canadian Manager*, *Chief Executive*, *Industry Week*, and *Vital Speeches*.

In addition to articles on the subject, research studies began to examine corporate performance with respect to social responsibility. The studies looked at an array of issues including variations in the socially responsive activities of firms, decision-making processes relating to public affairs, and methods for assessing social performance. The growth of interest in corporate social responsibility was evident by these various developments, and although it has waxed and waned with changing economic conditions over the years, the idea remains of enduring interest even in these tumultuous times. In the past few decades, many companies have been challenged with regard to their social performance not only by community activists but also by their stockholders. Perhaps most important is the fact that a self-interest function is served, since a healthy business needs a healthy community.

Mixing the Bottom Line with Social Responsibility

For business leaders the central dilemma is how to reconcile the bottom line with the desire to help solve social problems. While mixing these two concerns is not simple to achieve, it is possible.

This dilemma is the central theme of Tom Chappell's *The Soul of a Business* (New York: Bantam Books, 1993). Chappell, who ran a successful business, Tom's of Maine, felt personally dissatisfied with his total immersion in the business and decided to take some courses at Harvard's Divinity School. He became excited by the possibility of combining ethics and utility and decided to apply some of the abstract ideas he was considering at Harvard to the real world of business.

Chappell was particularly impressed by the views of Jonathan Edwards, an eighteenth-century New England philosopher, who proposed that people's sense of well-being comes not from being isolated and separate from their world, but rather from being connected to others. Chappell was interested in using this personal description as a metaphor for corporations, and he began to examine their relationship to their community and broader environment.

After struggling with how to balance corporate and social concerns, and making some mistakes by neglecting the profit margin, Chappell was able to blend a concern for economic return with social responsibility in his company. He recognized that unless he was concerned with the bottom line, any community efforts would not be successful. Chappell's approach was to educate and stimulate other companies to become involved in societal affairs and to "merge values with strategy." He emphasized that the total organization must be involved; the change cannot just take place at the top. He therefore called for a systems change and discussed in detail some of the elements that must be part of the process.

Another example of successfully mixing bottom-line concerns with corporate social responsibility is Shorebank Corporation, a commercial lending office in Chicago's impoverished West Side that lends money to poor and minority residents for the purchase or renovation of homes. Shorebank's president, Cliff Kellogg, who earned an M.B.A. from Stanford and is a Yale Law School graduate, wanted to work in a situation that "made a difference." The firm is not run as a charity; in fact, "return on equity has averaged 14 percent over the last decade, and default rates are on a par or lower than those for comparable lenders" (*U.S. News and World Reports*, Oct. 13, 1994, p. 105). The mix of bottom-line with social responsibility made the profits even greater than expected.

Changing Patterns of Corporate Social Responsiblity

The array of community-oriented activities of American corporations since World War II shows an evolving pattern of corporate social responsibility. In the early years, immediately following the war, raising money in the workplace for local charities became an established activity in industry, largely through fund-raising for United Way.

Since that time, corporate executives have served as volunteers on boards of social agencies—an activity that was viewed as a means of corporate advancement. More recently, corporate executives have expanded their activities and assumed diverse roles; some have loaned themselves to social agencies and others have served as consultants to help these nonprofit organizations develop more sophisticated managerial skills. In addition, some corporations have not only encouraged their workers to serve as volunteers in the community but have helped put these programs in place and provided supports and incentives for volunteering.

With the passage of time the viewpoints of corporate leaders regarding their community involvement have changed. Benefits to be derived for the corporation as a result of community involvement became clear and the quid pro quo in that relationship served all parties. For example, executives began to recognize the public relations benefits of being active in community affairs. At the same time, the corporate approach to giving shifted; whereas in earlier years corporate giving was a response to requests from different charitable groups, many corporations now link their giving to specific causes that further corporate interests.

This recent phenomenon, which is most relevant to our concerns, is one in which corporations expand the definition of corporate social responsibility by getting directly involved with the more complex social problems of society such as juvenile delinquency, unemployment, and poverty. This is new terrain for corporations, and their actions in these areas merit close attention and support.

Some Examples of Corporate Social Responsiblity

A broad array of private corporations throughout the country have accepted the notion of corporate social responsibility. The common thread among the various corporate programs is a commitment to becoming involved with current, complex societal problems. While many of the participants are major corporations, small and medium-sized businesses have also found creative ways to make a difference.

Entrepreneur John Steele and his wife, Lillian Kachmar, who run a small company, approached the challenge of becoming involved with social problems in a unique way. The couple decided that they wanted to employ welfare recipients since in their exploration of the welfare situation they learned that there was lots of training but few jobs available for welfare clients. Steele and Kachmar decided to expand their business, which manufactures coverings for outdoor furniture and decorative pillows. Working with public federal, state, and local agencies, they recruited and trained welfare recipients for the positions in their expanded business. Their focus was on women with dependent children.

Steele's experience and approach was noticed by the governor, who appointed him to a task force devoted to helping industries that are ready to hire welfare recipients locate public money for training. Training was seen as a critical factor and the first step in the process of moving welfare recipients into the workforce, since training results in less downtime among new employees. On a national level, it has been estimated that employers of welfare recipients save approximately $3,500 per employee after training and tax rebates.

IBM, one of the nation's largest corporations, has made a major commitment to the community. Tad Tuleja, in *Beyond the Bottom Line* (New York: Facts on File, 1985) highlights some of its activities over the years:

- The IBM Fund for Community Service supports civic, cultural, and scientific organizations.
- The company's Social Service Leave Program enables employees to take paid leaves of absence to lend their talents to public improvement projects.
- Through its Faculty Loan Program, IBM staffs colleges and universities that have large minority and handicapped student bodies.
- Through its Job Program for the Disadvantaged, the company lends equipment and supplies to local job-training organizations.

Several other interesting nontraditional approaches demonstrate the flexible arrangements that can be developed by corporations. Alternative structures are possible, including the sponsorship of nonprofit organizations. This approach is illustrated by the following examples.

The National Foundation for Teaching Entrepreneurship (NFTE) is a $4.5 million enterprise that offers a business curriculum in schools around the country. Steve Mariotti, the initiator of the program, was able to interest a philanthropist in backing his enterprise. With a $60,000 donation, Mariotti organized the effort as a nonprofit foundation. The program's success was noted in the national media:

> The program boasts 78 part-time instructors and almost 7,000 graduates—among them the founder of a thriving inner-city sports store and a rap-music company president. Many more than 2,600 low-income youths, many on welfare and a tenth of them former lawbreakers, are pursuing NFTE's mini "M.B.A."—a course that includes seed money along with the standard issue briefcase stuffed with workbook, entrepreneur profiles and calculator. (*U.S. News and World Report*, October 31, 1994, p. 103)

Children First, Inc., is a multi-million-dollar business, which was organized in Boston as an emergency child-care company, providing backup for working parents when their standard sitting arrangements broke down. The company, organized as a nonprofit, is meeting a vital social need and has expanded to serve employees of twenty-nine companies in three states. Rosemary Jordano, CEO, earns a five-figure salary but claims that her biggest satisfaction comes from getting employers to focus on family and child-care issues.

Another creative entrepreneur started Career Closet as a nonprofit agency to provide clothes for welfare recipients for interviews and jobs. Career Closet helps the women feel professional and "dressed for success." In addition to providing clothing, the agency offers encouragement and support on an informal basis. Although it is a nonprofit group with a large volunteer staff, Career Closet is relevant to our discussion because it creatively meets a real need as it contributes to the goal of helping welfare clients become employed.

There are various models and approaches to be tried. The challenge is to select a strategy that makes sense for and is uniquely tailored to each corporate entity.

The Changing Business Environment of Corporate America

There are many pressures exerted on corporate America and the nation is bombarded with news of the complex and critical societal issues that plague our country. There is at the same time a competing pressure brought about by the increasing globalization of national economies.

This shift to a global economy has had a direct, restricting effect on the potentially developing field of corporate social responsibility.

Robert Reich in *The Work of Nations* (New York: Vintage Books, 1992) notes that as the stakeholders of many American corporations are "turning into a large and diffuse group, spread over the world, [they are] less visible, and far less noisy, than national stakeholders" (p. 224). When American businesses were largely community-based, they were more directly influenced by local conditions, and competing interest groups and stakeholders in the corporation shared some common interests.

But in recent decades, as the United States has become part of a global economy, the local orientation and commitment of corporations has diminished; at the same time, stockholders are increasingly removed from the base of their investments. The benefits derived from community involvement in societal problems have become less obvious to stockholders and often it appears that their only concern is the return on their investment. This narrow viewpoint does not examine broader benefits to be obtained by the corporation. Consequently CEOs have become more risk-averse as they answer to their stockholders, in contrast to the likes of Carnegie, Ford, and Rockerfeller, who could unilaterally decide to contribute to the community.

The readiness of some executives and entrepreneurs to take the risk of mixing bottom-line considerations with social responsiblity reflects a broader view, one that recognizes that doing well is linked to doing good. This development deserves to be encouraged through our public policies.

Corporate Strategies for Welfare Reform

"Assuming your resources are not unlimited, how do you decide for one social project against another?" Tad Tuleja, in *Beyond the Bottom Line* (New York: Facts on File, 1985, p. 119), suggests that "different corporations define different areas of interest . . . , but most progressive firms seem to agree that at the heart of our current disequilibrium is chronic unemployment—and that this condition is intimately linked to a lack of appropriate education and skills training for America's 'underclass.' "

There are several approaches that corporations can take in becoming involved in welfare reform. The availability of permanent jobs is critical. Permanent jobs are a powerful motivator and incentive for welfare recipients who are eager to get off welfare. *Nightline* (June 19, 1994) interviewed several welfare recipients who were struggling to receive training in order to acquire skills to help them get jobs. They clearly wanted to change their lives and offer their children hope for the future. Unfortunately, the overriding experience of welfare recipients with employment is not only that is it difficult to get work, but the jobs they do get are often temporary or part-time; thus they are low-paying and without benefits.

A second major concern of those moving from welfare into the world of work is the care of dependent children. This concern is not limited to women on welfare; it is a concern of all families with children in which both parents are working. Day care is a job benefit available at the workplace in many European societies: the fact that corporations consider it a job benefit, and not a profit center, makes a difference. Day care is a societal need that can best be addressed by a partnership between the public and private sectors, especially when a primary societal goal is to get families off welfare.

There are many other small supports that employers can readily supply. A good illustration is provided by Patti Penny, who is involved in helping unskilled welfare recipients find jobs. Her company, Penmac Personnel Services in Springfield, Missouri, is highly successful, having grown from earning $14 million in 1993 to $22 million in 1994. Penny's success is due, in part, to a mother-hen-like determination to ensure the successful placement of her clients, which at times has meant supplying alarm clocks or workboots to participants in training programs.

If the welfare-to-work transition is to be achieved, corporations need to do some creative planning for work that simultaneously serves the company's interests as well as the interests of potential new employees. The efforts of employers and former welfare recipients must complement each other and not operate from an adversarial framework.

The issues raised here are important in a discussion of corporations and social responsibility. Though obviously not all-inclusive, they provide a start for serious examination of proposed steps to effectively deal with welfare reform.

Pennsylvania Blue Shield: The Case Study

The focus of this book is a welfare-to-work program designed by Pennsylvania Blue Shield. This major medical insurance corporation took seriously the challenge of corporate social responsibility by becoming involved in welfare concerns, but at the same time it needed to justify this involvement by its effect on the bottom line. In this respect, the company was typical of many other American corporations.

When Pennsylvania Blue Shield received a new contract requiring an additional workforce of approximately 500 people, it made the decision to recruit these workers in an unorthodox manner. It chose to collaborate with the Pennsylvania Department of Welfare and Department of Labor to obtain workers from the welfare rolls.

Pennsylvania Blue Shield's program is notable for its size and scope as well as for the results it achieved as it mixed bottom line considerations with corporate social responsibility. Pennsylvania Blue Shield was effective in training and employing over 200 former welfare clients, thereby lowering welfare expenditures and increasing income tax revenues. At the same time, the company met its objective of expanding its workforce to meet the needs of a project that generated additional income for the corporation. There is an array of unique elements of Blue Shield's program that warrant attention since they can contribute both to the design of public policy and to the involvement of corporations in welfare reform.

First, the program came about through the collaboration of the private and public sectors. Without public investment in the training program, Pennsylvania Blue Shield would not have become involved. And without the public provision of supports for the trainees in the program, the shift from welfare to work would not have been achieved.

Second, the operation was driven by the reality of jobs that were reserved for successful graduates of the training program. This is in sharp contrast to most projects of this type, which provide training but leave the quest for a job in the hands of the applicant.

Third, the number of people participating in the program was large. Pennsylvania Blue Shield hired 208 employees from the group of 242 who were trained. Most programs are much smaller.

Fourth, training was the cornerstone of the employment strategy and it was carefully tailored to the specific jobs to be filled. Pennsylvania Blue Shield provided curriculum materials and instructors from its standard training program, but the training was administered by a separate organization.

Fifth, top managers were committed to making the venture work. This intention was clearly transmitted throughout the organization, and the relevant staff from the organization were trained to work with this new cohort of employees.

Sixth, and most important, the results were dramatic. While the investment in time and money was significant, the benefits far outweighed the costs in all respects.

The varied businesses that recognize the importance of corporate social responsiblity in turning welfare clients into workers share some important characteristics. Above all the organizations' leaders are commited to making the job-training program work. Their programs are creative in responding to the problem of welfare, and there is some risk-taking involved in all of the programs, but all remain profit-oriented. They do not conduct the programs as charity. Further, they take advantage of linkages with public organizations and utilize public money for training. Finally, these businesses show compassion and flexibility in implementing the programs; they are ready to go the extra mile to ensure the success of their job trainees.

The experience of corporations in the realm of addressing social concerns is still evolving. Business schools are beginning to discuss corporate responsibility in their management curricula. Since this corporate thrust is new, it becomes all the more important to look at the experiences of individual companies that have had success in designing and implementing welfare-to-work programs.

3

How One Corporation Got Involved

This chapter describes one corporation's venture into the world of welfare. It tells the story of Pennsylvania Blue Shield, which sought to do good while doing well. In seeking to understand what led Pa/BS to become involved in the world of welfare, it is helpful to understand the many factors that created a receptive environment for the venture, allowing the organization to strike out into uncharted territory.

Jobs to Be Filled

The key factor in the initial readiness of Pa/BS to become involved with welfare clients was the organization's need for new workers. The company had just signed a contract with the Federal Health Care Administration to take over medical-claims processing for individuals enrolled in the Medicare Part B program in the state of New Jersey and consequently had 500 jobs to fill. It was of great importance both to Pa/BS and to the new pool of employees that these were seen as permanent jobs compatible with an extensive investment in training to equip new hires with a high level of speed and accuracy.

The environment in which the jobs had to be filled was a critical element in this story. The greater Harrisburg area was one of low unemployment. Since labor shortages were anticipated for the future, recruiting a new cohort into its workforce was a self-interest strategy for Pa/BS. Furthermore, the political climate was hospitable to a public-private partnership to train workers. In Pennsylvania, both the former Republican governor, Richard Thornburgh, and the then-current Democratic governor, Robert Casey, had promoted welfare-to-work programs in their efforts to cut welfare costs. Their strategies tied in with policies being developed at the federal level, and some programs were already in place at the state level to support the joint venture.

The Organization's Leadership

A second important factor that made this welfare-to-work venture possible was the commitment and interest of the management at Pennsylvania Blue Shield. Three of the corporate leaders were involved at the outset, and each contributed in a specific way: Sam Ross, president and CEO, had a clear philosophy about social responsibility and corporate behavior that underpinned the operation; George Grode, senior vice president for corporate affairs and assistant to the president, active in public policy matters, played a visionary role in the corporation in being externally oriented and seeking possibilities for community involvement; and Thomas Sommers, senior vice president for administration, the key figure in the actual implementation of the new program, was a risk-taker, ready to accept challenges and attempt innovations.

As is often the case with organizational change, an outside stimulus sparked a new procedure. At the end of 1987, Pete Krauss, who together with Grode had held key positions in the administration of Pennsylvania's former governor Thornburgh, initiated a meeting with Grode. Krauss was at that time a consultant on economic development and special advisor to Harrisburg's mayor to help the city's revitalization efforts. His focus was on problems of urban poverty. Although Pa/BS was located in Camp Hill, a suburb of Harrisburg, it was a major employer in the overall area, and Krauss thought that it might be in a position to work with its neighboring community.

The meeting was exploratory, to see where Pennsylvania Blue Shield's interests and needs could coalesce with Krauss's urban-economic agenda. The focus was on city residents, disadvantaged people, and self-help strategies. Grode, whose background included working with welfare families and job development for delinquent youth in New York City, was interested in this agenda and its potential contribution and laid the groundwork for the venture. Grode supported the proposal at that meeting; he suggested a meeting with Sommers since personnel matters were part of his responsibility.

Sommers was intrigued by the possible linkage between Blue Shield's workforce needs and the needs of urban Harrisburg. The ingredients of the proposed venture matched his interests and commitments. First, on a personal level he believed it was the right thing to do. Second, it was a venture in the human resources area where new manpower was needed. Third, because he perceived the program to be innovative, at the cutting edge of corporate-community relations, it created challenges for his leadership. He assigned the project to one of his staff to assess its feasibility. The response was an enthusiastic recommendation in its favor. It was here that welfare concerns moved into the private sector and corporate concerns interfaced with social need.

Within three weeks Sommers met with Grode to discuss implementation. Soon the project moved from being one of Sommers's many projects to being a "preferred project." In Grode's view, it was mainly Sommers's commitment that was responsible for the initiation of the program at Pennsylvania Blue Shield.

Sommers did a great deal of homework before he presented the ideas to Ross. He was prepared to discuss *why*, *when*, and *cost* as he made his presentation. A new dimension was introduced by Sommers at this time; he proposed that training be provided by Keystone Training Services, a subsidiary of Pa/BS, and funded by public monies.

In discussing *why*, Sommers emphasized that there would be clear benefits for both the corporation and Keystone Training Services. Blue Shield would benefit by having a training program with lower overhead costs; the program would also help the company comply with Equal Employment Opportunity mandates, enhance community relations, and involve little risk. The benefits for Keystone Training Services were even more evident: a guaranteed income with a smooth cash flow, a new area for expansion, increased visibility as a training site for other organizations, and last, but not least, an enhanced reputation in the community.

In discussing *when*, Sommers proposed a pilot project to last one year, from May 1989 to April 1990. The first year would test the feasibility of the venture and would establish procedures for continuing the program until all of the workers needed were trained and hired.

In discussing *cost*, Sommers believed that there would be no financial costs to the organization because the contract under the federal Job Training Partnership Act would provide the money for the training. Sommers thought that the anticipated revenue for the training might even exceed the direct expenses involved and cover some administrative overhead.

Although Sommers discussed the venture with Ross, it appears that the modus operandi of the company was based on a high degree of trust and autonomy. This assured that, unless Ross had a major objection, Sommers could go ahead with the program, and would be responsible for its success or failure.

From the outset, both Ross and Sommers anticipated several major returns on the Pa/BS investment. In the short run, the corporation would benefit since it could expect a return on investment within months after the trainees were hired. In addition, corporate taxes would be reduced through credits given for successful outcomes of the program. Furthermore, the corporation would be meeting a social responsibility by providing jobs to a diverse population.

Ross responded positively to the plan for other reasons as well. Not only did Ross respect Sommers's leadership ability, but the proposal was compatable with his own corporate philosophy and style of corporate leadership. Ross's philosophy helps to explain his readiness to work with the welfare system and is reminiscent of Tom Chappel's philosophy, which was discussed earlier:

> First, from a philosophical and political perspective, if we as a society view government as being too big, what are we willing to do about it? The challenges are there to meet the many social problems that exist. As a society we must take a constructive view now, and get involved, or we will pay for it later.

Ross termed this "a preventive strategy, a front-end strategy." He elaborated upon this notion:

> You either pay now or pay later. You can be involved with deciding upon the program and having input up-front as to how it will be shaped as opposed to paying later at the tail end through taxes, over which you have no control.

> Although people have negative attitudes toward welfare, they must be asked, "How would you do it? How much are you paying out now for welfare?" As we move into a more conservative era with the Republican ascendancy, if government funding is not there, we, as a society, still have to focus on need. What will we do? We cannot just focus on short-term fiscal problems.

In the long run, society as a whole is the beneficiary of job-training programs through reduced welfare costs and increased income taxes paid by the new employees. But the most important return is that welfare recipients are moving off the welfare rolls into the world of work, thereby enhancing their lives and joining the mainstream of society.

The critical actors at the top of Pennsylvania Blue Shield were committed to this venture and ready to take the risk. However, there were still several steps involved in obtaining agreement from the board of directors. Both Ross and Sommers made presentations to the board on an ongoing basis throughout the duration of the project. Before the go-ahead was given, Ross and Sommers clarified the legal issues involved. Since Pa/BS, through its Government Business Unit, contracts with the federal government to process Medicare claims, the question arose as to whether a federal contractor could engage in another activity that was not only involved with but dependent on federal monies. In February 1989 the legal department reported that there was no conflict of interest in what was being proposed. The department reported that it had

> ... thoroughly checked the federal materials available which include the Medicare contracts currently in effect between Blue Shield and the federal government, the Job Training Partnership Act and its regulations, and the federal Acquisition Regulations. None of these statutes or regulations prohibit a federal contractor from submitting a proposal to the government to supply services uner the Job Training Partnership Act as a subcontractor.

With the legal hurdles cleared and the rationale for the program clearly presented, the board of directors gave the go-ahead to the training program.

The Corporate Culture

Pennsylvania Blue Shield had decided to meet a corporate objective by working with an unorthodox work pool. Initially, the commitment to the new program was strongest in the top tier of the corporation, but skepticism was evident in other parts of the organization. For the program to be successful, however, the total organization had to be involved—a crucial factor in the program's development. The first training sequence and the first group to be employed would be critical tests for the new program.

The culture of Pa/BS had long included a willingness to innovate. Its leaders saw Pa/BS as a risk-taking organization, ready to venture into untried waters. As a nonprofit organization it was not risk-averse, certainly an advantage in this context. The fact that under state law the company had an obligation to make health-care coverage available to everyone regardless of their age, employment status, or health, already put it into a risk mode; it was only necessary to extend the risk mode into another arena.

The culture of the organization was shaped by Ross. With his strong community orientation, he expected all executives in the organization to be involved in community activity. This expectation permeated the entire organization, as evidenced not only by the fact that Pa/BS was the largest contributor to United Way but also by the fact that a large network of employee volunteers was involved in the community. Thus the seeds of corporate involvement in social affairs were firmly planted; the major difference here was that the new venture was on foreign soil, a new environment, that of welfare.

The corporate culture at Pa/BS was also affected by its existing relationship with the public sector. Since Pa/BS had had extensive experience with governmental programs, it had a clear perception of the benefits to be expected from such involvement. In this respect Pa/BS differs from many companies that do not have this experience and are reluctant to get involved with government programs because of concerns about paperwork, monitoring, and other general bureaucratic constraints.

The Commitment to Training

Another relevant factor to the readiness of Pa/BS to begin a welfare-to-work program was the organization's history of providing training to new employees to help them gain the skills necessary for competent job performance. The organization's commitment to training was evident in the active program it provided for the ongoing growth and development of all its employees. Pa/BS continually updated its training department to help its workers keep current with new technology related to their jobs, and also offered continuing education courses for personal growth. The corporation had always spent significant resources on training and viewed the training component as an essential part of its operation.

Getting involved in the training of welfare recipients was not viewed as a daunting task; rather, it challenged the corporation to expand its repertoire of training approaches. For the program to succeed, the work expectations had to be realistic and include opportunities for advancement. Pa/BS did not want to create a group of second-class employees. It was clear that a major training course would be necessary to prepare the welfare cohort for the job requirements. There was no question that the availability of public money for training was a big incentive for Pennsylvania Blue Shield to embark on this venture.

The training component was expected to be a critical factor in this venture and, as it turned out, required a major investment by Pa/BS, over and above the public funds available for training. The argument was made in the corporation that the program could be justified by the fact that training money was available and would reduce the costs, and risks, to the firm.

The Separation of Training from Employment

In the early conversations between Grode and Krauss, it was clear that Krauss was interested in having the site for the project located in Harrisburg and not in suburban Camp Hill, where corporate headquarters was located. His intent was to serve urban residents more effectively, especially since transportation would be readily available to an urban site and not to the suburban location.

Since Pa/BS was planning an expanded center for its training activities, it became evident that there would be a major benefit, for both the trainees and Pa/BS, in an urban training center. The trainees would benefit in several ways. First, it would be much more convenient to travel to a Harrisburg location. Second, and at least as important, the location would be less intimidating and more user-friendly than the Blue Shield headquarters, which are enormous and potentially confusing to a newcomer. From the corporate perspective, a separate training center would clearly differentiate the training program from the employment setting and create an arm's-length relationship between the trainees and the prospective employer. The hiring and employment aspects would be conducted at corporate headquarters in Camp Hill.

The entire job-application and hiring process was thus physically, as well as conceptually, separated from the training program. While the intent of the training was to prepare trainees for jobs that did exist, Pa/BS sought to protect itself further by retaining the right to review and select its hirees. Thus, it was made very clear throughout the training program that graduation from the program did not automatically assure a job. Nevertheless, all the graduates of the training program were hired. These training and employment processes will be discussed in greater detail later.

A final note related to location highlights the importance of involving as many segments of the community as possible when moving into the welfare arena. Although the building selected for the Keystone Training Center was a pleasant, user-friendly space that met many of the technical and financial needs of the training program, it was located in an area of Harrisburg that did not have adequate bus service. To ensure that participants could easily reach the training site, Krauss, in his role as consultant to the mayor for Harrisburg's revitalization effort, was able to arrange for better city bus services to the center. This illustrates the importance of community-wide involvement and investment in a project of this type, which requires an array of supports and services on many levels.

Collaborative Relationships

The involvement of other collaborating organizations in the project made Pa/BS feel further protected. Three other organizations became involved in the new venture at the outset, each having a clearly defined role: (1) Pennsylvania Blue Shield/Keystone Training Services was the trainer; (2) Creative Training Concepts provided the administrative apparatus; and (3) Susquehanna Education and Training Company (SETCO) was the source of fiscal support (see Figure 1).

Although Blue Shield prided itself on its commitment to training and the excellence of its program, its competence was primarily in technical matters; the company had no experience addressing the personal concerns and teaching approaches that would be appropriate with welfare clients. Thus, an initial concern in designing the program was to analyze needs of the trainees themselves in relation to the training process. Another concern was how the trainees would be selected. The aim of the project was to make a contribution to society and at the same time

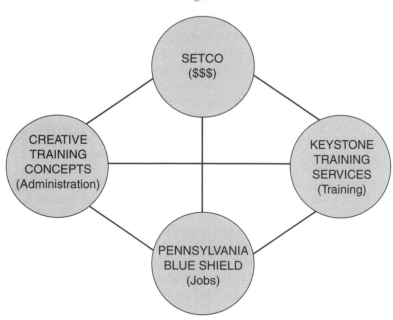

Figure 1. The Collaborative Relationships

ensure that Blue Shield's work would be done effectively. While the planners did not want to just skim off, or "cream," the best potential candidates, they knew they would have to exercise some selectivity.

Krauss suggested that these aspects of the plan could be handled by a Harrisburg consulting group, Creative Training Concepts, whose expertise was in providing specialized training approaches for special populations. This organization would also allow Blue Shield to keep the training process at arm's length by handling the program's administration.

The third collaborating organization, SETCO, played several roles. Before the Pennsylvania Blue Shield project began, SETCO was the organization that received proposals from private-sector corporations that wished to participate in federally funded training programs under the Job Training Partnership Act. Once it had selected Pa/BS, SETCO remained involved with the project for the duration of the training period, monitoring the use of public funds for services needed by the trainees (e.g., eye care, travel funds).

The interdependence of these organizational actors required extensive cooperation and collaboration. Each had a unique mission and a distinctive expertise which was to make the venture possible. The program was dealing with critical and thorny societal issues, involving different actors, competencies, points of view, and interests. All came together in this venture. The importance of a core of organizations with a stake in this process cannot be overstated. Sommers noted, "The business is broader than job creation. There are a whole array of factors: community infrastructure, transportation, . . . lots of pieces."

The centrality of the collaboration was recognized and clearly identified by Pa/BS. Each participating organization brought something to the table, and Pa/BS was not viewed as the deep pocket. Dave Rippey, director of education and training, was aware of both the leveraging and the buffering provided by the process, which brought with it a sense of equal commitment. Also, the risk of the project was shared by the different organizations.

Rippey put this collaboration in the context of a political process whereby each player needed the other. The government had a need to reduce welfare costs through the Single Point of Contact training program, Pa/BS had a need for workers, SETCO needed to ensure success in its selection of employers, and Creative Training Concepts needed to maintain its effectiveness and reputation. After both informal and formal negotiations between the four organizations, the program was launched.

The involvement of the local chamber of commerce would certainly have been an asset and would have helped to interest other local corporations in becoming similarly involved. Although the chamber did express some interest in Ross's initiatives, it did not make promotion of the program a priority.

In a description of this program it cannot be overemphasized how rare it is for a private corporation to yield any of its autonomy and decision-making in the conduct of its business. The readiness of Pa/BS to engage in a four-way collaboration highlights the importance of flexibility in the conduct of new ventures. In contrast, both Creative Training Concepts and SETCO, by the very nature of their missions, were always involved in interorganizational arrangements, since Creative Training Concepts provides expertise to other organizations and SETCO funds and monitors various training programs.

Summary

Various factors contributed to positioning Pennsylvania Blue Shield for its welfare-to-work venture: job availability, innovative corporate leadership, and a receptive corporate culture. These factors provided fertile ground for the new endeavor. The collaboration of several organizations strengthened Pa/BS in its readiness to take a major risk in a new arena. The supportive yet diverse roles played by these groups were critical in creating an environment that could yield positive results. Pa/BS did not feel it was out on a limb on its own. The involvement of public, non-profit, and corporate sectors, was a major factor in the success of this program. A final important factor in the development of this program was the arm's-length relationship created by the separation of training and employment, with separate locations for each.

This project was different from other Pennsylvania Blue Shield activities where the corporation normally retained full control of its actions. It required organizational flexibility to an extent not usually seen in corporate life, but such flexibility is essential in an undertaking of this kind.

II

TRAINING

4

Planning for Success

Since "the devil is in the details," this chapter focuses on the nitty-gritty specifics that went into designing the Pennsylvania Blue Shield program. Here we look at the program elements as described in the proposal for government funding and the financial considerations that influenced Pennsylvania Blue Shield to take on the project.

Formulating the Program

The details of the training program were developed during the preparation of the proposal that was submitted to SETCO. To obtain the federal money to pay for the training program, concrete and realistic decisions had to be made regarding the details of the program. Since the application process was competitive, success depended on demonstrating competence and commitment to meeting the program objective of preparing people for the job market. The proposal process also pushed the project to the forefront at Pa/BS, as it called for specific time frames for the planning phase and for the implementation of training activity.

The areas addressed in the March 1989 proposal included the administrative conditions for the project, an overview of the training program, entry-level criteria for the trainees, and a description of the jobs that would be available at Pa/BS.

Administrative Conditions

The creation of an arm's-length relationship between Pa/BS and the training program served as an important protection for the corporation, as discussed in Chapter 3. Creative Training Concepts became the contracting organization for the project, responsible for all the administrative aspects including hiring the staff, supervising the staff, overseeing the training process, preparing necessary documentation, and ensuring fiscal accountability. The contract was performance-based, and payment was based on the specific work peformed. All of these aspects of administration were given careful consideration in the initial contract.

The payment schedule, specified in the proposal, was spread over the one-year contract period. The rate of remuneration was based on the position of each trainee, with an average unit charge per participant of $2,600 for the 102 people to be trained. Thus the total funding requested for May 1989 through April 1990 was $265,200. Thirty percent of the total was paid per participant upon entrance into the training class, 30 percent upon midterm completion, 30 percent upon completion of the training, and 10 percent upon placement. If the Creative Training Concepts did not place the trainees within ninety days of the end of training, the final 10 percent was forfeited.

The staff positions that were needed to ensure a successful program were specified in the contract. These covered three types of functions. The first concerned administrative tasks and included an administrative assistant and a bookkeeper. The second concerned the training program itself. A program manager would oversee the day-to-day operations of the training program, a policy developer would be responsible for all policy issues that arose to ensure consistency in the program's approach, and a curriculum developer would prepare curriculum and supplementary material, create tests, and revise the curriculum as necessary. Three part-time trainers, to be hired by Keystone Training Services, would be selected from the Blue Shield training department on the basis of their expertise and experience in providing training for the specific medical-claims-examiner positions.

The third staff function covered was trainee-related. According to the proposal, a job counselor would be hired for the program to "be responsible for working with trainees prior to and after placement to assist with life difficulties experienced because of the demands of training or employment." In addition, a job developer would work to locate jobs for those trainees who did not meet the criteria for the Blue Shield positions. In fact, the proposal specified other related jobs for which this training would be appropriate, such as general claims examiners and claims-processing clerks. The relationship between the performance standards and the staffing picture was made clear by directly relating each position to the project outcomes.

Cost containment was evident in the efforts made to be realistic about this short-term project. For example, all equipment was rented or leased, and all staff jobs were part-time, limited to the one-year term of the contract but with the possibility of extensions from the federal government. The hiring for the project was a creative process, involving the maximization of different combinations and work situations. For example, the woman who was hired to be the program counselor was recently retired but had the exact combination of personality, experience, and skills required in this role. A part-time position met her needs while giving the project the benefit of her competence.

The Training Program

The training program was designed to train 102 people over the first-year contract period. The training period, which would last seven weeks, would be conducted in seven cycles. One important aspect of the training-program design was class size. The student-instructor ratio was deliberately kept lower than the standard situation to allow for more personal attention to the trainees. The ratio at Keystone was fifteen trainees to one instructor, in contrast to the standard situation at corporate headquarters where the ratio ranged from fifteen to twenty employees to one instructor. This small modification made a big difference.

The training program would prepare the trainees for the position of medical claims examiner using the technical content from the Pa/BS corporate training program for new hires. The thirty-five days of the seven-week training program were carefully outlined in the RFP packet and replicated the standard program:

> Participants will be trained in basic keying techniques, medical terminology and anatomy, and the use of the medicare claims examiner operations manuals. The training will take seven weeks. During the course period each trainee will become familiar with the operation of

an IBM CRT and the claims processing software. All training will be done on CRT units and software identical to those in use at Pennsylvania Blue Shield.

All of those involved in planning, however, recognized that the training could not be business as usual. Feedback from the trainees was incorporated into the process on an ongoing basis to ensure that the trainees were given every opportunity to learn the material, since they would be exposed to not only an entirely new body of knowledge but also a new learning and working environment. The opportunity for remedial assistance in learning technical material was also provided.

Care was also taken to ensure that on a weekly basis, and more often if needed, trainees could speak one to one with the instructor; the instructors made it clear from the outset that they would be willing to come in early, stay late, work through breaks and lunches, or whatever else it might take to provide assistance or remedial help.

In addition to opportunities for remedial work, special support would be available to deal with the personal situations of the trainees. Specifically, a job counselor would be on the staff to help with impediments unrelated to training such as child care and transportation.

The contract also specified completion standards required to be hired for the job of medicare claims examiner. These included a keying speed of 25 words per minute, the ability to process a standard number of claims per hour, and passing an exam on the medically related content areas.

An orientation took place for two hours before the training program began. The intent was to give the trainees an opportunity to get to know each other and the staff, and also to discuss some of the problems they could anticipate, such as transportation and child care difficulties. In later discussions when the orientation program was evaluated, staff members suggested that a one-week orientation would be more helpful and appropriate. This would allow for addressing the many loose ends that could have, and should have, been taken care of before the students started the actual training program. Appointments with welfare workers and other outside situations had caused absenteeism, which prevented the instructors and the students from concentrating totally on class content. As job counselor Betty Johnson expressed it, "Better pre-care was needed before the actual classes started." Taking extra time for orientation to address some of the personal difficulties that could arise is well worth the additional cost in pretraining time.

Entry-Level Criteria of the Trainees

One of the criticisms sometimes leveled at jobs programs for welfare recipients is that only the most likely to achieve are selected. Selectivity is valid, however, because it reflects most real-life educational and employment situations, which have criteria for entry. The challenge is to match the program with the individual so as to maximize the probability of success and make the work experience rewarding for both the new employee and the employer.

The planners of the Blue Shield program felt it was important to build in the possibility of early success. This would encourage not only Blue Shield but also future applicants to the training program, many of whom had had the prior experience of going through training and then not being able to obtain work. Since this program was distinctive in that training was linked to a large pool of job openings, the entry criteria were realistic and directly related to the available work. Thus, those who succeeded in graduating from the program were very likely to find immediate employment.

The entry criteria for the training program were as follows:

- A tenth-grade reading level as measured by the Test for Adult Basic Education (TABE)
- A typing speed of 25 wpm
- Completion of high school or concurrent work on a high-school diploma or GED
- A successful interview to assess the applicant's probablity for success based on attitude and circumstances.

In addition, anyone with a felony conviction or a drug-related conviction would not be considered, but those with misdemeanor convictions would be reviewed on a case-by-case basis. Applicants would have to complete an interest inventory, be able to work day or afternoon shifts, be able "to handle stress associated with production-oriented jobs," and be willing to work in a smoke-free environment.

SETCO was actively involved at the outset in selecting a larger pool of applicants from which Keystone could make its selection. For example, SETCO provided twenty-five names from which the personnel unit selected the fifteen who would be accepted as trainees. Sommers emphasized that there was some flexibility in the way the criteria were applied and that some risks were taken. For example, a candidate who did well in the interview but only typed 22 words per minute could be accepted. This was identified as a risk situation for Pa/BS because the candidate fell short of the demands of the job. There was also a risk for the trainee, who would be at a disadvantage at the outset of the work experience.

Since there was no flexibility in regard to the tenth-grade reading level requirement, SETCO would step in at such times and provide remediation through a GED program. SETCO also helped applicants who were not accepted into the Keystone training program get ready to qualify for the next round of Keystone interviews. The importance of a close collaboration between organizations that could complement and supplement each other's capabilities was especially important.

Jobs and Work Expectations at Blue Shield

At the outset the proposal had to document "how the training was designed and coordinated with input from local business, industry and labor organizations." The proposal clearly stated that "Blue Shield has experienced significant growth as a result of the acquisition of the New Jersey Medicare contract. Blue Shield is currently seeking other sources of employees for the position of claims examiner."

The proposal went on to make very clear that the new contract required a competent cohort of examiners and that Blue Shield was committed to having the employees become part of their permanent workforce. The careful attention paid to the training program, and the many special components inherent in the program (e.g., the creation of Keystone Training Services, the search for an appropriate training location) indicated its serious intention. It must also be noted that the pay for the jobs was specified at the regular pay scale for all beginning medical claims examiners, which was $7.13 at the start—a further indicator of the organization's interest in normalizing the situation.

The contract specified other aspects of the job about which the trainees needed to be informed. The jobs would be available either in the day or afternoon shift. The conditions of work were also specified. The positions required an understanding of the confidentiality of the work, the ability to work independently, and, most importantly, the ability to adapt to a frequently changing situation, due to the fact that Medicare rules and other aspects of the job are not fixed. The work setting was a small cubicle without a phone. Thus, it was clear at the outset that standard work for standard pay was the modus operandi.

Pennsylvania Blue Shield was prepared to hire all of the trainees who successfully completed their training, as confirmed in a letter to William Roberts, president of Creative Training Concepts, from Thomas Sommers (March 21, 1989):

> Pennsylvania Blue Shield will consider hiring graduates of your program. It is understood that the graduates, in addition to the requirements for successful completion of the program, would need to meet our hiring criteria as well. In other words, they will not receive preferential treatment over other applicants.

> Pennsylvania Blue Shield applauds your efforts in the development of job skills for individuals seeking to improve their employability. Blue Shield is ready to assist you in this worthwhile endeavor.

The contract also specified another aspect of the arm's-length relationship: a separate interviewing process for employment would be required, and the trainees would have to meet the usual hiring criteria for the position. The interviews for employment would take place at corporate headquarters in the Camp Hill location, thus giving a physical dimension to the move from training into the world of work.

As part of the performance-based contract, Creative Training Concepts assumed further responsibility for helping those students who did not complete the training for the position of medical claims examiner at Blue Shield to obtain employment elsewhere. Creative Training Concepts would help them develop the job-related technical and personal skills they would need to accomplish this goal. Thus the requirements of employment to meet the expectations of the performance-based contract were met.

Financial Underpinnings

As the public policy debate over welfare reform sharpens, the government's role in the funding of training programs to prepare welfare recipients for work remains a critical issue. The Blue Shield program is particularly instructive in this regard. If we look to the private sector, and not the public sector, as the source of jobs for welfare clients, with the intent of reducing welfare costs, then it is essential for the government to substantially assume the costs of training. Policymakers must be realistic about the capacity of corporate America to take on the risks involved in hiring welfare clients. The Pa/BS experience is particularly important because the company not only became involved, but was ready to hire hundreds of people into its permanent workforce.

The finance department conducted a careful financial analysis during the very early deliberations within Pa/BS. Training for the program was viewed as truly independent of the parent organization; it would be handled by Keystone Training Services, and budgeted independently. Thus it would be conducted in the same manner as any training facility would be, where return on the investment would be an important consideration. The revenues from the program, based on per capita tuition, would have to exceed the cash outflow. This excess return could also serve as a cushion to cover unanticipated costs.

Specifically, program expenses were calculated at $1,632.35 per participant for 102 trainees, bringing the total expenses to $166,500. This covered personnel, training equipment and materials, and rental, renovation, and maintenance of the training facility. The revenue for each participant was $2,100.00, bringing the gross revenue to $214,200. The return on the investment was thus projected at $47,700 for Keystone Training Services. Certainly, without the incentive of both a supported training program and some return on the investment, Blue Shield would have been less likely to undertake the project. It should also be noted that many services were contributed; for example, the salary of Keystone's director/project manager certainly exceeded the projected return and was viewed as an in-kind contribution.

Similarly the tax-credit program for employers was factored into the discussion. The benefits from this would accrue to Blue Shield after the new cohort of medical claims examiners became employed. Tax credits were available at both the federal and state levels. The Pennsylvania Targeted Jobs Tax Credit Program (1991) provided

> a Federal Tax Credit for up to one year to employers who hire employees from eligible target groups and can be provided concurrently with a State tax credit under the Employment Incentive Payment Program (EIPP) in cases where the employee is a member of target groups receiving General Assistance or Aid to Families with Dependent Children (AFDC).

If an employee works for 90 days or 120 hours in the year, the employer can claim a substantial tax credit—40 percent of the first $6,000 paid in wages. At the same time, the state tax credit is paid concurrently for three consecutive years of employment at a rate of 30 percent of $6,000 in wages in the first year, 20 percent of $6,000 in wages in the second, and 10 percent of the first $6,000 in the third.

For Blue Shield the gain from the federal tax credit was calculated to be $24,192 based on wages paid through December 1989. If the federal jobs tax credit were extended by Congress past 1989, and assuming that 84 new employees would start to work before June 30, 1990, Blue Shield would stand to get a tax credit of $100,800 in 1990.

While these tax credits provided significant financial incentives, they had another effect as well. The federal benefit reinforced the corporation's view that the enterprise was indeed a partnership between the public and private sectors to help solve a difficult and widespread social problem.

Summary

Although Blue Shield executives at the top level were interested in the idea of a welfare-to-work program, there is no question that it was the money available from the public sector for the training that got the project off the ground. Even though this was a corporation that had a very extensive and sophisticated in-house training department, the perceived risks associated with the new population, and the cost of a training program with special enhancements, were not costs the company was ready to assume on its own.

Perhaps of equal importance in the financial picture was the fact that the risks and commitments would be shared by three collaborating partners. Blue Shield, SETCO, and Creative Training Concepts had a different stake in the success of the venture. For example, SETCO's commitment was evident in its readiness to allocate more than half of its 1989–90 budget to the project.

These were indeed important and serious supports in a new and untried departure which Blue Shield was willing to embark on. However, there is no question that were the company required to go it alone, to take all the steps necessary to begin the program or assume all the risks necessary in either the training or employment of the welfare recipients, the response would have been different. Regardless of the corporate culture of community involvement and the positive risk orientation of company leaders, fiscal considerations were decisive.

Finally, the financial incentives offered by the government—namely, the funding available for training and the targeted jobs tax credits available to employers—were of critical importance. The program generated long-term savings to the taxpayer and a return on investment for the corporation. On a financial basis alone, the results were dramatic.

This chapter has focused on the underlying thinking that informed the design of the Blue Shield venture. It should be instructive in helping other companies understand both the incentives and the fundamental aspects of the program as they embark on their own ventures of this type. It should also be instructive in regard to public policy related to welfare reform.

5

The Importance of Staff

At least 13 area people have looked into the face of opportunity and seen it smile.

They are the graduates of a seven-week course Keystone Training Services. . . .

The graduates move on to jobs as claims examiners for Pennsylvania Blue Shield, Keystone's . . . corporate parent. . . .

Most are excited about graduating and going to work. "It means that I got an education and can move up in the company," says Dominique Shuttlesworth. The idea of computer training initially scared Shuttlesworth. "I thought I'd really fall on my face, but I did great. . . ."

("Opportunity: Training Course Boosts 13 Grads,"
Patriot News, 6/20/89)

What was it about the training program that brought about such an enthusiastic response from one of the trainees? Without a doubt the central characteristic that made the program a success was the quality of its staff. The competency of the people selected to work in the training program at Keystone Training Services was most impressive. It is not an exaggeration to suggest that this group was critical to the success of the training process. Among the staff members of the training program, the overwhelming feeling was one of deep satisfaction and pride in their jobs. The lessons from this experience call for examination of the personnel, their roles in the program, and what they learned from the training program. It cannot be overemphasized that any planning for replication must be particularly sensitive to the quality of the personnel involved. The investment made at this phase of planning will certainly be returned in the outcomes attained.

Another critical element in the program's success was the flexibility, or trial-and-error attitude, of those involved. The program could be described as somewhat schizophrenic in that contradictions and dilemmas were evident and had to be accommodated, and not always comfortably. This chapter describes some of the problems that arose as staff members strived to maintain corporate standards and at the same time give needed support to the trainees to ensure they would have the opportunity for success.

The route to success in this type of endeavor is not a straight path, but a circuitous one. But hopefully it will take you where you want to go.

The Project Manager

The position of project manager for the training program is a critical one for that person sets the tone for the entire operation. Pennsylvania Blue Shield found itself in a quandary almost as soon as the program began. The original manager, who was involved in selecting the site, designing the curriculum, and choosing the trainers, had resigned in the midst of the initial training cycle with the first group of trainees. To replace the project manager, Pa/BS appointed Gerry Rickards to be the director of Keystone Training Services and project manager. This was a major corporate contribution to the project, since in the first year the project manager's time was paid for by Pa/BS.

Rickards had been a training consultant at Blue Shield. As the top manager of the Keystone training program, he would play a key role in its success or failure. A retired military officer who began a second career at Blue Shield, Rickards had no experience in working with welfare clients and found himself highly challenged in the new situation.

When presented with this opportunity by Sommers, the senior vice president who had introduced the venture at Pa/BS, it was clear that serious risks were involved. Rickards would be leaving a secure position for the excitement and challenge of a new position; in his words,

> Maybe one of the reasons that I took the risks with the program is the confidence level that I have in Tom Sommers, knowing that he would not undertake a project unless he felt that there was merit, that it was worthy of undertaking, and that he had some vision of its success.

And a risk it was since Sommers indicated that Rickards' would be transferred from his original position and there was no guarantee as to what would be available once the training project came to an end, especially if it proved unsuccessful. Rickards recalled,

> With that in mind I was certainly motivated to do the best that I could. But beyond that motivation, the more I became involved with the clients, and saw situations and different environments that they came from, the more I became committed and the more I didn't want any of the students to fail.

Rickards set the tone for the entire program in several ways: he established a feeling of community in the training center, his approach was flexible; and, above all, he respected the trainees and was open to learning about a very different social group than the one he had been accustomed to working with. Rickards exuded warmth and acceptance, important attributes in his new role. His unusual ability to be supportive and flexible was highly respected by his staff as well as the trainees. His view of the trainers' role illustrates both his theoretical views and his personal performance: "The instructors had a counseling role as well as an instructional role. It was important to relate to participants on a personal as well as a professional basis."

As Rickards shaped the staff into a cohesive unit, a cooperative attitude permeated to all levels, and the trainees responded in kind. Having a small and separate site made it possible to create a close community and a special climate.

Selecting the Training Staff

The training program required special staff competencies related to the job requirements as well as the personal needs of the trainees. Blue Shield's training department was clearly focused on, and competent in, the technical aspects of the job, but a new area of expertise was needed to supplement that capability. Consequently, the staff complement was composed of several diverse components, all specified in the proposal written by Creative Training Concepts, the administrative arm of the project. The trainers from Blue Shield, on loan to Keystone for the project, were supplemented by special consultants who would train them in the nontechnical elements. There was also additional staff from other departments of Blue Shield to provide a broader orientation to the work situation.

The staff for the training program consisted of (1) the technical trainers for the medical claims examiner jobs, (2) the job counselor, (3) the job trainer for the personal issues of the trainees, and (4) the administrative personnel for the office and clerical functions. Special care was taken in developing the qualifications required of the staff who were directly involved with the trainees.

The technical trainers were recruited from the Blue Shield training department because they were knowledgeable and experienced in the training program given to all employees who become claims examiners; they brought the subject-matter expertise and the training-platform skills. Training staff were expected to be open, flexible, and helpful to each new cohort of trainees. Thus, applicants were expected to demonstrate sensitivity toward nontraditional populations.

Except for the possibility of a bonus based on the percentage of trainees who completed the training, no special incentives were offered to induce the existing group of trainers in Blue Shield's training department to take part in the new program. Rather, the opportunity to apply for these positions was offered on the premise that people should work in the program only if they wanted to. Interested applicants were attracted to the positions by nontangible rewards: opportunity for change, the challenge of a new job, and the chance to contribute to the company's broader goals.

Since the project was of short duration, special planning was needed at the corporate level involving the shifting of staff and the creation of temporary assignments. Blue Shield trainers worked at Keystone Training Services on a temporary basis for a period of one year, matching the time frame of the contract. When the training program was complete, the trainers were reassigned to their home departments at Blue Shield, and that those who had replaced them in their jobs for the duration of the project returned to their previous positions. It was expected that the trainers would remain in these positions for the time period specified, and would not apply for any new openings that might occur within the corporation. In short, Blue Shield management expected their commitment to be matched by the commitment of the selected trainers.

The selection of trainers was done by a panel of three people consisting of two training supervisors and a training manager from the human resources department of Blue Shield. Selection was a two-step process: each candidate was interviewed by the panel and then had to demonstrate his or her skills as a trainer in a one-day demonstration session. Thus the selection process was both competitive and demanding.

Eight people were identified as potential candidates by the manager of Corporate Training. All were either from the group of Medicare staff trainers or they were technical assistants from the medical claims area. All were highly experienced and knowledgeable about the technical tasks required of medical claims examiners. From the group of eight potential candidates, two trainers, Marge Janos and Steve Noss, were selected.

Staff Preparation

While Janos and Noss were technically competent and experienced in training traditional workers, they now had to learn a pedagogical style and methods of presentation that would be appropriate in the Keystone setting. They themselves had to go through a training period of several weeks, which was designed to prepare them for new methods of working.

The teacher training was handled by Creative Training Concepts, with assistance from the Department of Public Welfare. It included new instructional approaches such as the use of games and ice-breakers. More importantly, it included information about ethnicity, welfare, and different lifestyles and explored stereotypes that could influence the trainers' effectiveness. In addition, one day was devoted to giving the trainers information about the background of the trainees and doing problem-solving in relation to specific situations that might arise. The orientation included a discussion of problems that could be expected, including resistance to learning. This was the area in which the two trainers felt most insecure.

As the trainers were developing new techniques and approaches, they were expected to maintain the same standards used in training other medical claims examiners. Basically, the regular approach was enhanced by the new methods they had been taught, as well as by the tone of acceptance, support, and flexibility set by Rickards.

Curricular Approaches

Although the curriculum content matched that offered in the regular Blue Shield training program, the trainers rearranged the schedule to meet students' needs. For example, if the trainers noticed that students became exceedingly tired after the noon hour, they would move exams to the morning hours.

Furthermore, if the trainers sensed that the students were having a hard time and were just "not with it" one day, they would present more informal or less complex content on that day and postpone the more rigorous material for another time. Finally, if there was excessive absenteeism among the students on a particular day when important material was to be taught, they would rearrange the curriculum and offer less important content that day.

One small extracurricular change is also worthy of note. In the corporate environment at Blue Shield the trainers were formal in their dress. At the Keystone site they deliberately dressed casually to create a more welcoming and informal atmosphere.

Personal Growth

There is no question that the trainers grew and changed in their instructional approaches as the program progressed. As they became sensitized to the needs of the students and responded to the new situation, they were more effective.

The greatest challenge for the trainers was on the personal front as they learned how the personal dimensions of the trainees' lives could affect their performance. Staff members were eager to discuss their experiences in great detail, and all emphasized in various ways how striking and humbling the experience was, and how much they learned about the complex lives and impediments facing those in the program. It should be noted that all of the trainees were women—not an unusual picture in this employee pool.

The perceptions of the trainers mirrored the enthusiasm and commitment expressed by Rickards. Both Noss and Janos had felt insecure about their capacity to work effectively with welfare recipients, but their stereotypes of welfare clients broke down as they became engaged with their students. Noss expressed this clearly: "I bristle when I hear someone say 'just on welfare.' There are barriers upon barriers upon barriers that these people face."

The initial experience and her feelings as she entered the program were graphically described by Janos. Her language retains the intensity and flavor of her perceptions.

The first recollection is of our very first class that went through the program. Steve and I were going to teach the class together and because he had more experience than I did, he taught the first several weeks. He had to go away for a week and on Monday morning I was going to open up the Center. I got there bright and early before anybody came, because I knew a lot of people rode the bus, and they got there usually by 7:15 or 7:30 in the morning even though class didn't start until 8 o'clock. So I got there and I unlocked the door, and I turned on the lights and undid the alarm system. I was feeling pretty good about myself until I went back out to my car to get something I had forgotten, and when I came back to the door, I realized it had locked behind me.

Now we were all right outside waiting for twelve students to get off the various buses that they were going to come on, [and] it started to pour down rain. I realized that I was going to have to tell these people what a stupid thing I did. I wasn't sure what kind of a reaction I'd get from the folks. I didn't know if they'd be angry or upset, or really how they would take it. However, before I knew it, I was standing under an awning with twelve students and they started to tell me about situations that had been embarrassing in their lives. We were laughing and joking, and it turned out to be the ultimate ice-breaker. By the time we got into the building we were kind of a happy group. I realized that they were just like any other folks and they had gone out of their way to make me feel comfortable. I guess we bonded in a way that I didn't think was possible.

You have to realize that some of these ladies got up at four o'clock in the morning to get themselves ready, to pack lunches for their children, and to take their children to school or daycare, sometimes on the bus, sometimes by cab. They had a lot of things to face, a whole lot more that I did in the morning. All I had to do is get up and get myself ready. They had already been up for hours and must have felt like they had already put in a whole day.

It could have been a kind of ugly scene out there when they discovered that I couldn't let them in the door, but instead it was really positive. Everybody felt good and laughed, and I sometimes see one or two of those individuals and we still laugh and joke about it. It was a good way to get broken in.

The trainers became sensitive to meeting the individual needs of the women and helping them cultivate a sense of worth—an important element in this training process. In a small but significant gesture Janos and Noss held a birthday party for each trainee. The party would usually be held in the morning. All would sing, the honoree would receive a gift-wrapped mug, and Janos or one of the trainees would make a birthday cake. The event was personally meaningful for the student and also demonstrated the community spirit which was shared among the staff in the training program. In the words of Rickards, "It just gelled, we all pulled together. We were all committed and we really worked well as a team."

The Job Counselor

Like the trainer positions, the job counselor position was given a high priority and was viewed as a particularly sensitive one. The importance of this position is evident in the description provided in the proposal:

> The job counselor will be responsible for working with trainees prior to and after job placement to assist with life difficulties experienced because of the demands of training or employment. The major goal is to help ease the transition of the individual into the workforce.

The person in this position would act as a facilitator and gatekeeper while keeping the interests of both the potential employees and the employer at heart. The effectiveness of this position would be reflected in the ability of the trainees to complete the program and be ready for the world of work. The candidate had to be sensitive to the needs of the women, accepting of their differences and their circumstances, nonjudgmental in attitude, and nonthreatening in style.

The job counselor would focus on the supports needed and the transitions of the trainees in the context of preparing them for the expectations of the training program as well as the realities of the working world. The proposal specified that the counselor would give assistance with the personal problems of the trainees that could impede attendance or participation in the training program: "This philosophy of service and caring enables participants to focus their full attention on the training at hand."

Betty Johnson, who had spent twenty-five years doing training in corporate development, was hired to be the job counselor on the project under the Keystone Training Service structure. Johnson was not a member of the Pennsylvania Blue Shield staff, and the autonomy of her position allowed her a great deal of discretion in how to use her time. She reported to Rickards, who supported her decisions about her work.

Johnson had an unusual perspective on her position. In her view she had a distinct advantage in not being a counseling professional because the women in the training program felt more comfortable coming to her, an ordinary person, with their problems. She was both effective and innovative in the many roles she played in this program.

Johnson acted as an advocate on behalf of the women in several unique ways. First, if there was no public transportation available for them, the women received an allowance of $1,200 from SETCO to buy a car. Johnson negotiated with several local car dealers to sell the women the cars even before they were able to pay the full amount. She used Pa/BS as the psychological guarantor in the negotiation. Second, Johnson negotiated with the car insurance agents to issue policies to trainees on an installment plan. Third, she negotiated with landlords to wait several months before raising the rent when the women shifted from trainee to employee status.

Finally, Johnson even negotiated with the Department of Public Welfare and SETCO. Two examples are worthy of note. The women often did not have adequate clothing for the week; Johnson presented this need to the Department of Welfare and a clothing allowance was provided: $75 at the start of the training program and another $75 the first week at work. Many of the women also did not have the eyeglasses they needed to do their work; Johnson helped to arrange eye examinations. Since the state provided only a small allowance for the exams, a doctor had to be found who would honor that amount. Johnson contacted the Society for the Blind to find appropriate eye doctors.

As the main person dealing directly with the personal needs of the trainees, Johnson was seen as supportive, encouraging, and helpful. At the same time she was very firm and direct with the trainees about what was expected of them in the training program. Her expectations matched the expectations found in the employment setting. First and foremost, the trainees had to be punctual. If they were late once, they were given a warning; if they were late twice, they were removed from the program. This was a tough regimen for women who had few backups or supports in their home situations. Consequently, Johnson spent a good deal of time discussing backups, including how to deal with emergencies. She stressed that it was essential to have more than one fall-back strategy in case the first alternative, or even the second, fell through.

However, it must be noted that exceptions were made in those situations where the trainee was highly motivated and had potential to succeed. If unusual circumstances created the problem, Johnson, together with Rickards, exercised discretion in applying the rules.

Johnson's unique role is further illustrated by other unconventional approaches. If a trainee did not have enough money for the bus and was eager to come to training, Johnson would pick her up in her car. In another case, one trainee was habitually late. Johnson subsequently learned that the woman's boyfriend would not permit her to leave in the morning until she had satisfied his immediate demands. Johnson interpreted the problem financially for her by costing out the time lost. This explanation helped the trainee set her priorities, and Blue Shield's willingness to be flexible regarding the rules when necessary enabled the trainee to stay in the program.

These examples demonstrate how Johnson went the extra mile in flexibly and creatively interpreting her role. Not only was her assistance critical in meeting the day-to-day needs of the trainees, but it gave them a strong sense of support and confidence, which helped to empower them to take charge of their lives. The personal problems of the trainees, which were anticipated in detail by the designers of the program, were multiple and complex, but Johnson was never discouraged by what might appear to others to be roadblocks. There was no problem that Johnson did not attempt to resolve. She was also an effective advocate for the trainees with other agencies and with the community at large.

Summary

This chapter has described the personnel considerations and organizational perspectives that went into the preparation and execution of the training program. While it is important to set overall content goals and standards for performance, the standard curriculum cannot be slavishly followed. It is clear from this experience that the trainers need to be sensitive and intelligent in their approach, ready to change both the content sequence and teaching methods as appropriate. The corporation also needs to be flexible in its expectations and willing to give supports that extend beyond the classroom. There is no standard formula for success; the only uniform prescription is that of ensuring a flexible and responsive approach that is user-friendly and recruiting staff who are caring, committed, flexible, and open to learning.

6

A Win-Win Game

Gerry,
  You couldn't do
  such nice things
  if you weren't
  so nice yourself!
  Just wanted to thank you for the opportunity to go through this
training and *also* for letting us go to Camp Hill. You'll never know
just how happy you made us three girls from Lebanon!

The positive response of the trainees to the Blue Shield training program is poignantly captured in this message to Director Gerry Rickards
from three graduates of the program. It illustrates one of the outcomes
of the program having to do with relationships and personal growth. A
description of what happened to the trainees who completed the program is appropriate here as is a discussion of the program outcomes in
view of costs and savings. Pennsylvania Blue Shield's data demonstrated
a dramatic return on the investment in training.

The Trainees

Eighteen groups, each consisting of 12 to 15 trainees, completed seven-
week training programs at Keystone. As of October 1993, four and a
half years after the inception of the program, a total of 242 people had
participated in the training.

  Pennsylvania Blue Shield's original intent was to draw trainees not
only from the welfare pool but also from among the pool of unemployed,
dislocated, or underemployed workers. The actual cohort of trainees, as

it turned out, was primarily welfare recipients: 229 welfare recipients were referred to the program, whereas only 8 dislocated and 4 under-employed workers took part. Furthermore, although men were included in the recruitment process, the self-selected group of participants consisted of women. This result may be related to the criteria for the position, especially the requirement of typing 25 words per minute.

The group was diverse in terms of racial composition; of the total trainees, 112 were white, 126 were black, and 4 were Hispanic. The trainees ranged in age from 18 to 47 years old. Figure 2 shows the age distribution as of 1992. Given that this is indeed a young population, with 83 percent 30 years of age or younger, it is clear that this investment in training offers a potential of many years of return in the workplace.

All the participants were originally expected to have at least a tenth-grade reading level and either a high school diploma or its equivalent. These criteria were somewhat flexibly applied; if a woman was in the process of obtaining a high school equivalency diploma, the high school

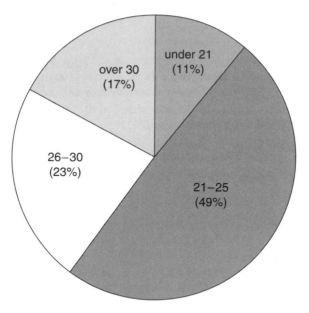

Total Participants: 242

Figure 2. Ages of Training Participants, June 1992

requirement would be delayed. As a result, some of the trainees received their GEDs while in the program.

Employment Status upon Completion of Training

Pennsylvania Blue Shield was very pleased with the outcome of the training program in terms of the number of trainees that graduated and were hired by the corporation. Of the 242 women who had entered the training program, 208 trainees (86 percent) completed it (see Figure 3). Only 34 individuals dropped out of the training program or were not continued primarily due to absenteeism or chronic tardiness. Pennsylvania Blue Shield hired all the graduates as they completed their training over the four-year time frame. As of January 31, 1993, 115 of the 208 graduates (55 percent) were still employed in the corporation.

Table 1 presents the retention rate as well as the number of months of employment for graduates in the eighteen training groups. As of October 1993, 96 program graduates were still with Blue Shield. Fifty-

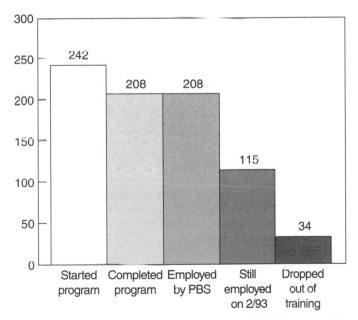

Figure 3. Training Completion and Placement, June 1989–January 1993

Table 1. Keystone Training Center Claims Examiner Skills Program: Retention Statistics (A/O October 1, 1993)

Class Number	Initially Employed	Currently Employed	Months Employed	Retention Percentage
1 (June '89)	13	4	42	38
2 (Aug. '89)	12	3	40	58
3 (Oct. '89)	13	6	38	46
4 (Nov. '89)	13	4	37	31
5 (Jan. '90)	13	5	36	38
6 (Mar. '90)	11	5	35	45
7 (May '90)	14	5	33	36
8 (June '90)	14	5	32	43
9 (Aug. '90)	13	5	30	46
10 (Oct. '90)	11	5	28	55
11 (Nov. '90)	8	3	27	50
12 (Jan. '91)	11	7	25	73
13 (Mar. '91)	7	6	23	86
14 (May '91)	11	6	20	64
15 (June '91)	9	7	19	89
16 (Sep. '91)	13	5	16	54
17 (Nov. '91)	12	9	14	92
18 (Apr. '92)	10	6	10	100
Total	208	96		46

1989—51 Hires, 22 Currently employed (43%)

1990—84 Hires, 37 Currently employed (44%)

1991—63 Hires, 46 Currently employed (73%)

1992—10 Hires, 10 Currently employed (100%)

Report date: 2/10/93

three were employed elsewhere, bringing the total number of those who had completed the training program and who were still employed to 149 (72 percent).

Since much of the debate on welfare reform centers on the number of years a person can be on the rolls, it is of interest to examine the history of the welfare recipients in this program (see Figure 4). Of the original group of 208 graduates from the training program who were hired, 195 (94 percent) had been welfare recipients. Fifty-five percent had been on welfare for less than two years; the balance (45 percent) had been

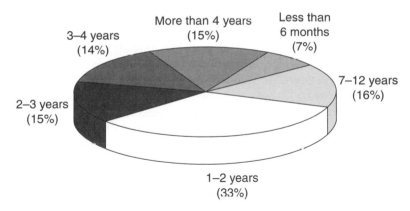

Total Trainees on Welfare: 195 (94%)

Figure 4. Welfare History of the Trainees

receiving welfare for more than two years. It is significant to note that when given the benefit of a training program, all the women were able to take advantage of the opportunity, successfully complete it, and obtain employment.

A Cost-Benefit Analysis

A cost-benefit analysis of the training program can be approached in several ways: from a financial perspective, a corporate perspective, and a human perspective.

The Financial Perspective

The data compiled by the corporation show a substantial return on the investment in training. In its financial analysis Blue Shield asked three questions: (1) What were the savings to the welfare program for the women who were no longer needing support? (2) What was their contribution to the tax base as a result of their earnings? (3) What were the tax credits earned by Blue Shield?

The direct savings that resulted from the training program between

1989 and 1992 are shown in Table 2. For an investment in the program of $655,266, the savings to the public coffers were indeed dramatic. More than $2.4 million was saved in welfare support payments over the four-year period during which the training was conducted and the graduates were employed. In addition, the tax contributions made by the women who were now off welfare and gainfully employed totaled more than $1.2 million. In addition, there were indirect financial gains as well. The tax credits to which Blue Shield was entitled for this period totaled $430,492. There is no question that all parties benefited financially from the investment in the training program.

This venture would not have been possible without the government's up-front investment in the training program of $655,266. Even with this government support, both Pa/BS and Creative Training Consultants contributed indirectly to the total program costs, and program expenses exceeded reimbursements from government agencies (Table 3). Pa/BS's expenses over the three contract periods were $676,166; Creative Training Concepts' expenses were $170,396.

The Corporate Perspective

Through the welfare-to-work training program, Pennsylvania Blue Shield found an avenue for expressing further its civic-mindedness and sense of social responsiblity. The caring orientation of many of its employees was enriched and broadened as a result of this program.

Pa/BS also benefited from its participation in the venture in terms of public relations. Keystone Training Services received recognition

Table 2. Direct Savings from the Claims Examiner Training Program, June 1989–June 1992

Date	Cumulative Welfare Savings	Cumulative Tax Contributions
12/89	$ 121,567.00	$ 70,973.21
12/90	708,860.00	352,434.99
12/91	1,043,190.00	552,531.55
6/92	532,650.00	322,511.51
Total	$2,406,267.00	$1,298,451.26

Department of Public Welfare Investment $655,266

Table 3. Costs of Claims Examiner Training Program, June 1989–June 1992

Reimbursement		Expenses			
Commonwealth (DPW Contract)		Blue Shield		Creative Training Concepts	
1990 (1st Contract)	$269,818	1990	$282,193	1990	$48,984
1991 (2nd Contract)	$255,917	1991	$191,744	1991	$77,120
1992 (3rd Contract)	$129,531	1992	$202,229	1992	$44,292
Total	$655,266		$676,166		$170,396

at both the state and national level. At the state level it was honored with awards from both the Department of Education and the Department of Welfare of the Commonwealth of Pennsylvania. Secretary of Welfare, John White recognized Pa/BS for its distinctive performance by placing it on the Department's New Directions Employer Honor Roll for "outstanding cooperation with the Department to help train and employ Pennsylvania's most vulnerable citizens and thereby directly contribute to their achieving a fuller measure of independence and dignity." Pa/BS also received the SETCO/PIC Recognition Award as the Oustanding Classroom Training Contractor in 1990 as well as the Outstanding Program Award from the Pennsylvania Directors of Community Action.

At the national level the corporation was also highly visible. It was nominated twice for the U.S. Department of Labor and Industry's LIFT Award, and although it did not win the award, Blue Shield received public acknowledgment and a citation. Furthermore, Blue Shield was cited in a study conducted by the University of California at Berkeley for the Department of Labor and Industry as one of the top ten training programs in the country.

By participating in the training program corporate leaders at Pennsylvania Blue Shield became invested in the effort to get people off welfare and into the working world. Furthermore, the experience served as the basis for further ventures into community-oriented activity on a corporate level. Pa/BS actively started new community outreach programs as it made its facilities available to community-based groups. Specifically, staff from groups in various communities had access to the computers in the company's three learning centers, which are located in communities away from corporate headquarters, and could master skills to more effectively perform their administrative work. Not only could they learn computer skills, or upgrade existing skills, but they were exposed to databases and different software packages. In addition, there was a ripple effect as the new knowledge was passed on to participants in their programs.

Finally, and of critical importance, the experience with the training program made the leaders of Pa/BS much more aware of the realities of an outreach program and the need for the corporation to be flexible and ready to provide necessary supports to ensure the success of all outreach activities.

The Human Perspective

It was indeed exciting to note the changes that took place among the women who participated in the program as they entered the mainstream of society. Not only were they no longer on welfare and no longer stigmatized by that status, but these changes also benefited their children. Program manager Gerry Rickards expressed sensitivity to these changes in his comments concerning the participants of the program.

> Many of them had been told they can't do anything, that they're losers, and that they might as well not even try. One of the things that is concerning is that when they started to do good and started to feel good about themselves, there would be family members who would put them down, who were very jealous. They did not always have the family support that you might think they would. . . . All of a sudden these submissive young women, who did whatever they were told, started to feel good about themselves and started to have self-esteem.

The gain in empowerment for the women was noted by all the staff involved in the training. The staff was also aware that they themselves had benefited from the training experience, they had broadened their outlook and their capacity to work effectively in the program.

Summary

The debate concerning welfare reform usually centers on financial issues, namely the costs of the welfare program and the potential tax savings if the program is cut. Seldom are the human benefits to be derived from an enlightened welfare policy considered. And very rarely are the benefits of corporate involvement in societal concerns discussed.

This chapter demonstrates that positive outcomes can be obtained on all three of these dimensions. But the successful outcomes are clearly predicated on an initial outlay and investment by the public sector, from which all else flows. It was clearly stated by all the key actors in the organization that the corporation would not have undertaken the venture had the training program not been subsidized by government programs. Although the corporation was ready to make commitments for the employment of several hundred graduates of the training program, that action was contingent upon the fact that it would not also have to pay for the costs of providing quality preparation and training for the jobs.

7

Trainee Perspectives

The more I became involved with the clients, and I saw situations and different environments that they came from, the more I became committed and the more I didn't want any of the students to fail, ever. I always tried to give them the most that I could in terms of being sensitive to their needs and sensitive to their situation. I always tried to encourage, and did whatever it took. If I had to go get somebody, if I had to take somebody to the doctor, whatever it took to help these folks get through. What I had always thought, and certainly was proven wrong rather quickly, was that with anybody on welfare, they are probably there because they can't learn very well and things like that. I found out that they are just as capable as anybody else given the chance and given the encouragement. (Gerry Rickards, Keystone Training Services)

In this chapter we shift our focus from the corporate and organizational aspects of the training project to the women themselves—their motivations, their perceptions, and their problems. This project offered a unique opportunity to examine the realities of the lives of the women seeking to leave the welfare system. While the difficulties the women faced led to some pitfalls for the program, which created stress for all parties, many of these could be avoided with some additioning planning. Weaving together the comments, perceptions, and views of the trainees, the staff members, and Pa/BS executive staff, forms a consensus that reflects an awareness and sensitivity to the realities of the trainees' lives and the consequences of these realities on the program. The coalescence of views can pave the way for smoother transitions in future programs of this type.

Entering Training

A critical aspect of any welfare-to-work program, and one that requires careful attention, is the entry point into training and out of welfare. In the case of Blue Shield there was no active advertising for the program due to the fact that in the initial year of the program, recruitment was by referral only, which was conducted by SETCO. The selective recruitment was intended to ensure a successful first year for the program, which would make its continuance possible.

The trainees saw this limited access as a shortcoming. Some found out about the program accidentally; others felt they really had to search for it. Furthermore, rather than being encouraged by their welfare case workers to aspire to professional development and potential growth, the trainees reported that their counselors were often discouraging, making comments such as "Are you sure you want to try this?" or "You'll lose WIC benefits" or "Who is going to watch your kids?" The trainees felt that it is essential for welfare caseworkers to make their clients aware of training and employment opportunities to encourage them to aim for success.

After the initial group of trainees had graduated from the training program, information about the program spread by word of mouth to other welfare recipients. In this way interest in the program grew among welfare recipients. For example, one woman, Anne, who wanted a full-time job with the prospect of a permanent situation, heard about the training opportunity through her girlfriend. She had never held a job because she married and had two children right out of high school; after her divorce she found herself on welfare. Anne herself initiated contact with the training program and was tested and accepted. She had a great feeling when she arrived at "this neat training center."

Another trainee, Joan, was excited about the prospect of training for a medical claims examiner as a way of fulfilling her dream of taking her children to Disney World. This was the first program she had heard of that could make her dream possible, and this goal served as important motivation for success.

At the outset of the application process for the training program, applicants were given clear information about the program, including expectations of trainees and possibilities of employment. They were advised that while jobs were available, and were reserved for graduates of the training program, they were not guaranteed. The applicants knew they had to qualify for the positions. The crucial point is that from the beginning they also knew that positions that they could fill existed and that the attainment of a job depended on their ability and their commitment. This situation was very different from some of their past experiences where they had gone through training and then found there were no jobs available. The possibility of stable employment was a major inducement to apply for and succeed in the program.

The importance of motivation and commitment is illustrated by the experience of one of the women in the program. Jane was not accepted initially because she did not meet the entrance criteria for reading level and typing skill. At SETCO she was very insistent in expressing her desire to participate. Sensing her serious intentions, the SETCO representative asked Rickards to interview her. Jane was interviewed but did not qualify and was not accepted in this first screening. Nevertheless, her motivation stimulated her to upgrade her reading and typing skills and eventually she was accepted.

Even so, Jane had some more work to do in order to succeed. The job counselor at Keystone made it clear that she had to be a team player on the job, and that some of her aggressiveness would work against her in the employment setting. Determined to succeed, Jane modified some of her unacceptable behavior and four years later was employed at Blue Shield and, according to Rickards, was considered to be a very good employee—"a compliment to the program and specifically, a compliment to herself and her abilities."

The trainers at Keystone, Janos and Noss, estimate that 90 to 95 percent of the the women who participated in the program wanted to be there. They were highly motivated and were determined to succeed.

Perceptions of Training

As the trainees moved through the program at Keystone Training Services, their views of the program evolved with their experiences. The women's views on the training process were obtained in two ways. First, a meeting was held with a group of women who had completed the training and were now Blue Shield employees; then, six follow-up individual interviews were conducted with employees from this group.

When asked what made it possible for them to stay in the training program, the participants gave several answers. Most important was knowing that there was a job at Pa/BS when the training was complete; as one trainee said, "If you succeed in the program, you are guaranteed a job." Until this time the experience of many of these women was that after training jobs were either just not available or, if available, were short-term, part-time, or dead-end. This new context was very motivating for the trainees.

Several additional factors were identified as necessary components of the welfare-to-work program. These are not presented in order of importance. All of them offered support to the trainees and enabled them to remain in the training program.

The specific services provided by SETCO were mentioned as playing an important role in the transition from being on welfare to the training situation. The child-care support, clothing allowance, and eyeglasses provided by SETCO were all cited. Some appreciated especially the allotment of money for transportation costs. In rare cases, when public transportation was not available and where there were no alternatives, a small allowance made it possible to purchase a used car.

The quality of the instructors in the program was deeply appreciated by the participants. They were described as being "great" and "very thorough." One woman said, "They knew their job, they cared, they gave extra time, and extra tests." The women were clear in their understanding that if one of them did not make it through the program, it was the individual's problem, not the trainer's, since the trainees were given the help and special attention they needed.

The training itself was experienced as very challenging. The fact that the training environment replicated the actual office situation, while difficult at times, was recognized as being an important preparation for employment. The training program, in addition to providing specific skills, was very effective as a transition from a nonworking, welfare status to a working status.

When asked about what special difficulties they encountered on a personal level, several of the trainees mentioned "professionalism" and "attitude adjustment." One woman said she had not known how to interact with others or how to handle her problems and frustrations without becoming defensive or hostile. The women learned how to respond to criticism on the job while remaining calm and clearly focused.

From the trainees' perspective, what made the entire program work was the fact the Rickards and his staff were like a family in providing emotional support. They sensed that the staff wanted to see all of them succeed. If the trainees were not adequately motivated in the early stages of the program, Rickards and his staff gave them the little push that they needed—something no other training program they had been involved with had ever provided.

It is noteworthy that although the applicants did not know what their potential for employment was, they started the program because they did have the goal of leaving welfare. Those who progressed through the program had the willpower and determination to succeed.

Dealing With Personal Problems

The personal problems that affected the trainees' participation in the program were stressful and often overwhelming. These problems are not usually understood or appreciated by the public at large. Becoming educated about these aspects is a prerequisite for developing policies and programs that are appropriate for welfare recipients. While some of these realities cannot be dealt with easily, many of them can be handled with up-front awareness of the situation and an exploration of possible strategies to remedy the problems.

To begin with, one of the unexpected and unnecessary barriers facing the women was the routine workings of the Department of Welfare. The department was accustomed to having welfare recipients available for appointments at its office during regular business hours. This created a severe problem for the trainees because these hours were the same as the working hours of the Keystone training program and Keystone had firm expectations about attendance. Meeting the attendance requirements of the training program was essential if the candidates were to graduate and be eligible for future employment. As a result, special arrangements had to be made with the Department of Welfare for the women to get their support checks and their food stamps at other times.

An additional problem related to the operation of the Department of Welfare was the dispensing of reimbursement funds to the trainees. Often vouchers were not prepared in a timely manner. As a result, the women were usually short of money for transportation or babysitters. Often the sitters would be ready to quit because they were not being paid on time. One woman was in the sixth week of the seven-week training program before she had received any money. Two women commented that the funding problem was a "nightmare." One said, "It got to the point where, because of these special needs, I did not think I was going to be able to stay in the job training program."

In spite of the fact that the Department of Welfare was a major player and collaborator in the venture, it was not sufficiently supportive during the implementation of the program. From the trainees' perspective, those who succeeded did so because of their own willpower and determination, often in spite of what they perceived as the welfare office's discouraging attitude toward the program.

Another major impediment was transportation. The women in the program were, in Grode's term, "transportation dependent." They could not control this essential factor that was directly related to the demand for punctuality on the job. If there was a car in the family, it was generally not available to the trainee; either it had to be shared with a spouse or with others who were in command of the schedule and did the driving. Furthermore, if the vehicle was shared with others, they usually did not have the same commitment to a schedule that the trainee did.

If the trainee depended on public transportation, she could still have problems. If something unexpected happened in getting the children off to school, a trainee might miss the bus, which only came once an hour; or if there was a major snowfall, which happened in the area with frequency, the public transportation might not come at all.

The transportation problem was an acute one that affected many of the women in the training program. Both Johnson and Rickards served as emergency drivers on various occasions when the problem was not the fault of the trainee and when the trainee had called in to explain the situation. Johnson was particularly concerned if a test was being given that day in the training program. Thus, for example, if a woman could not come into Keystone because her welfare check had not come and she did not have bus fare, Johnson went to get her; if a snowstorm canceled bus service, Rickards went to get her. This immediate and concrete assistance was a clear demonstration of the staff's eagerness to see the trainees succeed, especially since there was little allowance in the program for lateness or absence. The first time a trainee was absent she was warned, the second time she was removed from the program.

The problem of wardrobe can be a major one for women on welfare. Many have only one outfit that is appropriate for work, which must be washed and ironed daily. If the outfit has been prepared for the next day and nearby pipes burst and soak the clothes, the trainee is stuck. Such situations really did happen. Counselor Johnson did negotiate with SETCO to have a clothing allowance available for the women. To be able to dress appropriately both for the training course and the work setting, they received $75 during the training period and another $75 upon employment. The importance of appropriate clothing was emphasized by several trainees, who believed that wearing a suit was related to success. Without the special allowance they could not have afforded to buy a suit.

Women who are attempting to get off welfare and into the world of work have family pressures placed on them that many middle-class workers are not aware of. Often they are viewed as the responsible family member in an extended family situation that can include several generations with many dependency needs, both physical and emotional. In addition to the demands made by family members are those made by many of the agencies that interact with the family. Welfare agencies, mental health agencies, and the schools all use these women as their point of contact. One 32-year-old woman, for example, had a sick, elderly parent with many complex medical needs, as well as two children with their own sets of demands. It is not simple to manage such a burden while seeking to leave welfare and maintain a job, especially when one cannot afford backup help.

Often the housing available to welfare clients is not conducive to a stable and orderly life. The household can be chaotic and the housing itself in poor condition. When heating costs rise, an entire apartment building can lose its heat if other tenants in the dwelling have not paid their bills. If on some nights the family must all sleep on the floor in the kitchen near the oven, sharing blankets to keep warm, how rested can a woman be when she goes to work the next morning? The trainee's sleep can also be disturbed by noise or violence in the home setting.

When the housing situation deteriorates further, mothers worry about the effects of high crime neighborhoods, gangs in the streets, and dangerous folks in the hallways. In such situations, the mother often has to accompany the children home from school or make an arrangement so that the children are not alone. This is above and beyond the problems associated with making child-care arrangements during the workday.

At the same time, the children may be having a difficult time in school and need extra help. If extra meetings with school personnel are needed, the mother must attend as the sole responsible parent. Furthermore, the school tends to use a stable individual as the contact not only for her own children but for other children related to her, adding yet another burden to an already overburdened day-to-day life.

One final burden for the women in the training program was the emotional upheaval that comes with changing one's status. The trainees were, as all of us are, part of a family and social network. Their attempt to move out of an established status was usually met with great resistance in their immediate environment. Family members as well as their peers on welfare may resent and resist this new development.

One trainee, for example, in accepting the need to be time-oriented, brought clocks into the house and began to wear a watch; she was heavily criticized for her concern with time. Other women also experienced criticism from their peers on public assistance as they took steps toward employment; they were seen as taking on airs or acting as though they were better. This kind of negative social interaction sabotages the back-to-work efforts of the welfare population. There is simply no support within their social network for their struggle for upward mobility.

The incentive to earn more money to better the lives of one's children was a powerful one for the women in the program. For women coming off welfare, however, the switch to a working life brings short-term drawbacks. During the transition the children have fewer material things than their classmates, and they are often stigmatized and less accepted in the classroom setting.

On the other hand, having a working mother offers some important benefits to family members. One of the women interviewed pointed out that her stable work situation definitely had an impact on her three teenage children. They were learning by watching her and had become more disciplined after noticing their mother's newfound discipline in preparing for the next day's activities. They were watching less television, getting more sleep, studying more, and starting the day with a good breakfast. The woman was proud to report that her daughter now had a part-time job.

Janos, on the training staff, expressed the view that advance planning for the day-to-day realities of women on welfare could have prevented some of the problems in the training program:

> Poor class attendance was often a problem. Tardiness and absenteeism were frequently the results of poor planning by the students or the agencies they had to interact with. Students should have abeen able to concentrate on what they were being taught. Instead they were constantly confronted with other issues which either took them away from class or worried them to distraction while they were in class. These things should have been worked out prior to the start of class.

Janos reiterated the pressing problems noted above as she highlighted child care, transportation, eye care, welfare appointments, and clothing. Having this knowledge beforehand would make all the difference in effective planning for training. Although not all the eventualites could have been predicted, certainly some of the problems could have been mitigated. For example, the demands of other agencies upon the lives and schedules of the women could have been adjusted to avoid a double bind, where the women were expected to be at two places at the same time.

There is no question that the day-to-day demands on women who seek to leave welfare and enter the world of work are extraordinary. There is also no question that this transition would be impossible without adequate supports to make it happen. Rome was not built in a day. The transition period cannot be hastened and impediments must be addressed realistically if success is to be achieved.

Responses of the Training Staff

The experience of working directly with the women in the training program had a great impact on Rickards, the program manager, and on Janos and Noss, the trainers. Since Rickards played a critical role in creating the supportive and effective Keystone environment, it is instructive to hear his description of the changes he experienced:

> I always thought that people on welfare were there because they wanted to be and they weren't capable of doing a lot of other things. I thought that most of them could do some kind of menial labor and I was very disgusted that people would receive welfare rather than work, and because of the program, I found out an awful lot of things. The stereotyping that I was involved in, of course, is very commmon. . . .
>
> What I found out was that people on welfare could be me, could be my brother, my sister, my son, my daughter. It all depends on what

has transpired in our lives. A disadvantage here, or making a wrong decision, or just being in the wrong place at the wrong time. I found out that people on welfare are just as smart as anybody else. . . . They know they can provide for their families a lot better by being on welfare than having a menial job and not having skills to market. . . . And I know that [by] providing people with an opportunity they start to believe in themselves, they can accomplish about anything that they want to.

. . . I found that there were many everyday crises in their lives that they had to contend with that made them so much stronger than a lot of people I know. And that they could still deal with these crises and still get on in life. I found that a lot of these people are very strong, they're strong-willed and have a strong disposition because they are compelled to be that way. But many of us would never make it.

Rickards emphasized how committed the trainees were to the program and how great their desire was to obtain work. One of the trainees needed gallbladder surgery as soon as possible, but she declined to have the surgery until after she had completed training so as not to threaten her standing in the class. Another young woman, who was in the first group of trainees, did extremely well and became an informal mentor to other women in her class. Her contribution was recognized, and once she started to work at Blue Shield she was brought back to subsequent training classes to give briefings about the work environment and what the trainees could expect.

Janos and Noss echoed Rickards's remarks concerning the impact the program had on them. They were deeply invested in the venture and eager to be effective in their roles. Both Janos and Noss recognized that this was an altogether different experience and they were open to learning. They were anxious about their ability to communicate and work effectively with the participants. The bottom line for Janos, with all the complexity inherent in the situation, was the value of the program and the growth experienced both trainers and trainees. Her feelings emerge in the following vignettes.

Working with the SPOC program was very rewarding. Most of my experiences were good ones; however there were a few that were not so good. . . . Generally, a good rapport was established early on between instructor and students, although sometimes it took a bit longer.

Personalities could affect the direction the class would take. If you were fortunate, you might have a "leader" type of student who had a really positive attitude. This would have a great effect on the other students. Peer pressure is a reality and if you're pushed in a positive way, the results can be wonderful. However, if your "leader" type has a negative attitude, it can be devastating to a class. I experienced that at least once, and it was an uphill battle all the way.

There were some challenging situations I encountered during my years with the program that were memorable for me. Once, two students fought over where they were going to sit. I tried my best to resolve the conflict but failed. They simply refused to respond to my direction. Finally the student who had the seat first offered to move. It was a bit frightening and very embarrassing.

There were occasional small outbursts of racial tension and a few problems with students of different age groups. The majority of the time, however, it was amazing to see how well these people from vastly different backgrounds and age groups got along. They got to know each other and knocked down some barriers in the process. It was a real learning experience for all of us.

Graduation

Several aspects of the program facilitated the transition from the training situation at the small and familiar training site in Harrisburg to the employment situation at the large corporate headquarters in Camp Hill.

Over the training period, different people from Blue Shield came to the Harrisburg site to meet with the trainees. These meetings played a major role in the socialization process and facilitated communication between the trainees and the human resources staff.

Initially, Senior Vice President Tom Sommers provided the official welcome to the program from the corporation's perspective. To follow up on this contact, members of the human resources department were actively coming and going to make themselves known to the trainees. Through these contacts the trainees were exposed not only to corporate dress and style but also to corporate language and conversation. Even with these attempts to bridge the gap between the training environment and the work setting, one of the women in the program left after one week of working in the company because she was overwhelmed; she did return, however, and is still working for Pa/BS.

The graduation exercise was an important rite of passage, which also played a major role in affecting the transition. Graduation took place in the afternoon of the final day of the training program. A full meal was provided by Blue Shield, and family members were invited to attend. Representatives from all of the collaborating organizations were also present at each of the graduations. Members of the media also attended. SETCO awarded each of the graduates a certificate of completion. In addition, Blue Shield gave each graduate a calculator, and the job counselor gave each graduate a notepad and pen. Graduation was a deeply meaningful event for the participants, and a festive one, too. According to Rickards,

> These graduations were so special and some [graduates] were so emotional that all of the [audience] had tears in their eyes. When these young ladies would come up to get their certificate, they would say "This is the first thing that I've ever completed in my life" or "My parents (or family) will be proud of me now" or "I want my kids to look up to me, to know that education and training is important."

Rickards went on to say that being involved in the welfare-to-work program was "the most memorable experience of my life. If I never do anything else, nobody will ever be able to take this away from me, the significance of being part of a project as this."

Janos also had some special recollections about the graduation ceremonies. In particular, there was one graduation day she would never forget:

> We always tried to have a graduation ceremony on the last day of class. . . . We asked each girl to come up front to get the certificate, and I would be up front and so would Steve [the other trainer] and Bill Roberts from Creative Training Concepts, and whoever else might want to say a few words. This one particular student got up and as she came up to get her certificate, she shook my hand and then she asked me if she could say a few words. She explained to a packed house, for some reason that day we were overflowing with people, that she wanted to thank everyone that was involved with the program for helping her to achieve her goal of getting her certificate and getting a job. She explained that she had had to drop out of high school because she was pregnant, and then she went on and had, I think, two other children after that, and had gone on welfare to support herself and her family. She explained that her mother had been on welfare before her, and her grandmother before that. She was so thrilled to have been able to break the cycle. Actually there were tears stream-

ing down her face as she explained to everybody that to her this was like the graduation day she had never had. I'll tell you, there wasn't a dry eye in the house when she was done. I think that everybody involved in that whole program knew that day why they were involved and were proud to have been part of helping somebody to achieve a goal like that. I'll never forget it as long as I live. Of course, I bawled my heart out as well, and I think I'm sure that I was not alone. It was a proud day for everybody.

The graduation exercise recognized the completion of a demanding course of study in the face of great personal odds. And its significance was magnified by the fact that persons from all the organizations involved with the project, representing the larger society, came to the event to recognize the graduates' achievement.

Summary

This chapter has provided a picture of the lives of the women who entered the program. It has focused on the obstacles that must be overcome and the supports that must be provided in order for candidates to be able to participate in the culture of the work world. Those who are ready to enter into training are already motivated. The availability of jobs is a critical factor in encouraging trainees to complete the program. At the same time, the training program and the support services were perceived by all the women as a crucial factor in preparing them for the big step from welfare to work.

III

EMPLOYMENT

8

Integrating the New Workers

Three senior corporate executives at Pennsylvania Blue Shield had become committed to the venture from the outset. Once the training program was in place, Blue Shield itself had to begin preparing for the new cohort of workers. The specifics of the work situation, the preparation of supervisory staff, and their perceptions and recommendations all had to be addressed. In short, management faced the complex process of adjusting the culture at corporate headquarters in suburban Camp Hill to accept and work with the new employees.

Corporate Culture

While policy set by leadership at the top, conceived by a few actors, was necessary for the inception of and commitment to the venture, it was not sufficient for successful implementation of this new corporate program. Until the employment phase of the program, the only corporate contact with the training program in Harrisburg had consisted of bringing in key managers from Blue Shield to help orient the trainees to their future work setting. This had taken place away from the corporate Pa/BS setting and the required acculturation process had not yet occurred.

The next phase in the venture on the part of Pa/BS was handled by a key actor, Senior Vice President for Government and Corporate Business, Everett Bryant. In this phase, in which the trainees moved from

88 *Employment*

training to work, hired trainees were placed in Bryant's operation center. Tom Sommers introduced the venture to Bryant, who was responsive and ready to help with the implementation process in the medical claims area. In Sommers's view, Bryant's positive response to the new work program grew out of the environment of commitment, support, and trust among the senior executives at Blue Shield. Bryant saw the venture as serving Pennsylvania Blue Shield's social objective of giving people opportunities and encouraging and promoting diversity. He operated on the assumption that "at the same time that you are managing a social program, you also feel a responsibility to both the government and to the public." Very mindful of the risks and challenges in this situation, Bryant took a pragmatic approach. He noted the fact that Blue Shield was in a competitive environment where price and quality were critical elements. In his words, "If these people wouldn't meet our standards, it would be a failure."

Even with these reservations related to the bottom line, Bryant proceeded in a direct and committed manner to see that the employment phase was implemented by those employees who would be directly involved with the new workforce. He informed the supervisory staff in no uncertain terms that "this is what we are going to do—no ands, ifs or buts." It was up to the supervisors to see that the frontline staff cooperated. The major challenge and burden fell to the Human Resources department, which had to create the climate and conditions that were necessary for the acceptance and inclusion of this new cohort of workers.

Some supervisors were originally skeptical and resistant; they were fearful that they would have to keep the new workers in their units regardless of their competence. They felt threatened by this possibility since they had production schedules to meet and were responsible for their unit's productivity. But when the supervisors learned that the expectations for performance would be the same ones applied to all workers, and that the expectations were high, they were relieved and more ready to participate and be cooperative. The new employees, like all new employees, would have a probationary status. They would be expected to perform or they would not be retained.

Bryant clarified the supervisors' roles: "They were not to single out these new employees: those who were successful would do so on their own, like new immigrants needing to assimilate." Even so, some adjustments had to be made since Pennsylvania Blue Shield is a very large company and any new employee can get lost, especially an employee with little experience or exposure to the world of work. For example, Pa/BS has clear and specific requirements of its workers: employees are assigned specific lunch hours, coffee breaks are scheduled, workers must obtain permission to leave their workstation, and workers are expected to meet production expectations. For employees unaccustomed to the atmosphere of a large bureaucracy, with the associated rules and regulations, this can be a most disorienting experience.

Bryant further emphasized that the moment of entry into the corporation was a critical point and that the organization could not view the new situation as business as usual for several important reasons. First, the attitudes of some frontline Pa/BS employees were not acceptable in regard to welfare recipients and the challenge became one of creating a hospitable working environment. This required some change at the front line. Second, the new employees had very different social skills, attitudes, and life experiences from the traditional Blue Shield worker, which would unquestionably require special supports.

The supervisory staff played a critical role in this situation as they counseled the frontline staff and helped them to cooperate. It had been made very clear to the supervisors that there was a major commitment to this program on the part of the corporation and that there was no choice: they themselves would have to cooperate and they would have to get all the frontline staff, whom they supervised, to cooperate as well.

Given the deeply embedded attitudes about welfare in the general population, and in the Pa/BS workforce, it was clear that intensive and special attention needed to be paid to these aspects at the outset if the experiment were to prove successful. All this was in the context of a complex work task: the work expected of the new employees was extremely difficult in terms of both medical language coding and technical computer work. (Later in this chapter, when we discuss the perceptions of the supervisors, it will become clear that the message they received was ambiguous, which made it difficult for them to operationalize.)

This entire procedure was unusual for Blue Shield in that a new group of trainees was being inducted into the organization in a manner that was different from the usual recruitment and hiring procedure. But Pa/BS sought to insure that all the new employees would be employable and would have attained the expected entry-level competency.

According to Bryant, two major aspects of the initial employment experience are important to note for any organization embarking on a similar project. First, all of the program employees came into the organization at a single point of entry, so supplementary supports and strategies could be focused on one particular area of the organization. This made the transition both intensive and manageable. It would have been a much more difficult process to manage if the employees had entered at numerous departments.

Second, the fact the Rickards was a member of Blue Shield's staff as well as director of Keystone Training Services provided essential continuity between the training and employment phases of the program, as well as special insights into the situation. Rickards was actively involved in collaborating with the supervisory staff at corporate headquarters while serving as director of the training program in Harrisburg. He understood the many special needs of the trainees, had learned what was helpful to them, and of greatest importance, had their trust.

In Bryant's words, "patience and understanding were essential throughout the process and throughout the organization," especially since, as discussed in the previous chapter on the trainees, their personal problems could be overwhelming.

Specific Work Issues

Much thought was given to how to incorporate the new employees into the Pa/BS organization. A strategy was put in place by Sommers and Bryant to reserve and hold 15 positions for each of the training groups. This would result in a cumulative total of 102 positions. It was important that the positions be designated and held in reserve for the trainees; otherwise, the jobs could easily be filled through the normal hiring process, since it would take a full year for the total complement of trainees to be ready to enter the work situation.

The capacity of Pa/BS to accommodate this large a group was made possible by a new contract awarded by the federal government to process claims for Medicare enrollees residing in New Jersey. At the same time, the company was large enough to allow for assimilation and mobility of the new employee group. The possibility of upward mobility was an important factor in motivating the new employees; they did not feel relegated to the bottom level of the organization. The situation would certainly not be attractive for the new workers if they felt stuck in one place, nor would it encourage positive attitudes toward their work or the corporation.

One other aspect of the work situation affected not only this new group of employees but Pennsylvania Blue Shield employees in general. Although the company runs a child-care facility, the Carefree Learning Center, Inc., it was not a resource utilized by women in entry-level jobs because the fees were too high (Pennsylvania Blue Shield operates Carefree as a profit center, and not as an employee service or benefit). The fact that this resource existed and was not a practical option for the new employees created tension for the women in this project. This was also a problem in the organization at large, in which many employees are single parents, since running a child-care facility is not economically feasible without sufficient private fees or public subsidies.

Preparation of Supervisors

The director of continuing education, Donna Cheatham, was also a critical figure in the implementation of the program. The supervisors reported to Cheatham and she was very clear regarding her responsibilities and expectations. In her view, the commitment of senior management was the necessary ingredient in making the jobs program workable since this group established the framework for the entire project as well as expectations for all the other levels of staff. Each staff level had to give careful thought to how it would carry out its new charge.

Everyone who would be working directly with the new employees needed to gain an understanding of the new population that would be entering the organization. Such understanding was of particular importance for supervisors since they would be working with the new employees from the moment they entered the workplace. Because the supervisors would be the people involved in on-the-job training, acculturation, and the evaluation of the new employees, they were central in getting it all to work.

Cheatham was charged with the selection, orientation, and preparation of the supervisors who were to be involved. She recognized that supervisors would serve as important role models for the workers. To help ensure that supervisors would be motivated, she asked for volunteers, rather than drafting people, to take on the responsibility. She interpreted the new supervisory role as an opportunity for personal and professional development; the supervisors would strive to empower a new cohort of workers, foster their self-confidence, and help create op-

portunities for them. Cheatham believed that many people are motivated
to be helpers and that this experience could provide that opportunity for
those who were so inclined. In addition, it would be an opportunity for
the supervisors to prove themselves for possible promotion in the corporation.

The first task was to bring stereotypes concerning welfare recipients
to the fore, to acknowledge that they exist, to explore the implications
of these stereotypes, and to recognize the necessity for growth and
change concerning these negative views. The most common stereotype
was that all welfare recipients were shiftless and lazy, and this stereotype had to be broken down.

Cheatham noted that not all supervisors were fixed in their views or
accepted this stereotype; some were open-minded, but some were not.
Cheatham dealt directly with these attitudes and expected to change the
supervisors' behavior. She would ask supervisors to put their concerns
on the table, and then explore why "it is a big deal now when it is not
a big deal with other workers." She expected her supervisors to give the
workers a fair shot, so it would be clear that if they did not succeed, it
was not because the organization failed them or made them uncomfort-
able enough to inhibit their performance. "The lack had to be the person's, not Blue Shield's," she noted.

A major part of the orientation process for the supervisors included
helping them to understand the obstacles facing the women in the program. This was indeed a new vantage point; the circumstances were unfamiliar to the supervisors. For example, they had to learn how to help
the employees develop contingency plans for transportation or child care
so that a family emergency would not affect their workplace attendance
or performance.

Although the problems faced by the program participants were discussed in the chapter on the trainees, they were new realities for the supervisors. For example, workers might need to be helped to schedule
doctor's appointments after hours so as not to use up their vacation time
for this purpose, and might need to have two or three back-up people
in case normal child care arrangements failed.

Cheatham noted that a particularly important part of the orientation
program for supervisors concerned their role in dealing with serious personal problems. She emphasized that the supervisor would serve only
as an information and referral source. If, for example, a worker was bat-
tered, either physically or emotionally, the supervisor would arrange im-

mediate counseling through the employee-relations department, rather than get involved in the problem directly. Supervisors were instructed to minimize the amount of information they received about employees' personal problems.

The importance of flexibility, and the dilemmas and contradictions that were experienced, were noted in Chapter 5. There is no question that there were conflicting goals between the corporate standards and the needs of the new employees to be supported to provide the opportunity for success. It was important that Cheatham was able to use flexibility in administering company policy, especially during the first year of employment, during which most adjustments took place. This flexibility related to both personal needs and the work situation. Cheatham suggested to the supervisors:

> Try to build up confidence; do not crush them by focusing on mistakes made in their work. Use verbal, not written, interaction as the major means of communication. Focus on the worker's role and support their efforts to stay on the job. In regard to the personal needs, instead of the normal two days of sick leave, allow more time. Be flexible in relation to productivity expectations.

An important part of the supervisor's role was to help the new employees become acculturated to the work ethic, which was expected of all workers and necessary for successful employment and advancement in the corporation. The supervisor could also play a critical role in the development of an appropriate work style and work manner. The supervisors were encouraged to reinforce the positive aspects of each worker's performance, such as arriving at work on time, dressing appropriately, and taking initiative on the job.

Perceptions of Supervisors

There were two types of personnel dealing with the entry-level workers: the supervisors, who were involved with personnel and administrative issues, and the technical assistants (TAs), who dealt with medical and insurance details. Because the supervisors were the linchpins in the process, caught in the middle between the broad objectives of upper management and the day-to-day realities of working directly with the program employees, their views are especially important.

The supervisors attended a series of meetings with their managers and the employee relations department, during which the expectations and objectives of the project were explicated. Emphasis was placed, during the initial period, on understanding the new employees' backgrounds and being sensitive to their needs, while at the same time expecting standard output in job performance. The message regarding flexibility, however, was never clearly understood by the supervisors, a reality that created a great deal of stress for them. For example, the new workers showed excessive absenteeism, which was caused by the complex problems in their lives. Such absenteeism was not to be tolerated in the work setting, and the supervisors were on the horns of a dilemma. On the one hand, the new employees were not to be treated any differently than anyone else; on the other hand, the supervisors were expected to be sensitive to the special needs of these women. In effect, it was expected that two masters be served during this initial period of employment.

Not all of the new employees required extra attention; many performed competently and without personal distractions from the outset. But others had personal problems that often went beyond the experience of the regular workforce, such as court issues, boyfriends in jail, and battering and abuse. The supervisors felt unprepared and inadequate to deal with such situations As a result the new employees often turned to Rickards, from Keystone Training Services, rather than to their work supervisors for support. They had established a relationship of trust with Rickards and knew he was sensitive to their concerns. In these cases Rickards always called the supervisor to inform them of the situation and to relocate the solution of any problems to the worksite. In these instances there was also some follow-up by SETCO from the counselors who were working with the women.

The supervisors also looked to Rickards for the concrete support they themselves needed, since it was not forthcoming elsewhere. Rickards's constant input and concern with the program was very important. The supervisors felt appreciated when he called them; his interest also encouraged them to be helpful to the new employees so they would succeed. In part, they wanted to be able to tell Rickards that all was well. This relationship served as a major incentive for the supervisors, especially since they received no other recognition of the complexities and challenges of their new roles. While internal expectations of high performance on the job did motivate the supervisors, they appreciated the additional reinforcement because of the extra problems and challenges they faced.

The supervisors believed that, although upper-level managers felt there were adequate supports for them to help with the employees' problems, the corporation was, in fact, not adequately equipped to deal with all the issues. They argued that more preparation was needed at all levels, including concrete guidelines for themselves about "what to do and how to do it."

In spite of the new challenges, and the associated problems, the supervisors highlighted the fact that the quality of the work performed by the new employees was the same and often surpassed the expected standard performance of workers hired in the more usual manner.

The other staff level group that was involved in the project was the TAs, who serve as a buffer between supervisors and frontline staff to provide closer, hands-on supervision and technical assistance. They do not have supervisory status but help the employees with the nuts and bolts of their jobs as medical claims examiners. Tension developed at this level since the TAs were not adequately prepared for their involvement in the project. They never had a view of the whole program and had not been appraised of the special needs of the new workforce and the need for a sensitive response. As a result, they treated the program employees in the same manner that they treated all employees. For example, if a TA heard that a worker needed eyeglasses, a usual response would be "Okay, so what's different?" Lacking the preparation that was given to the supervisors, they did not walk the extra mile or show flexibility in dealing with the new employees. The TAs did not understand the pressures facing the group of women.

It was the TAs who were most involved in the assimilation of the new employees into the organization. The work setting at Blue Shield was more stringent in its demands than the environment at Keystone Training Services, where an informal dress code and more flexible scheduling were allowed. Consequently, the demands of the corporate setting were often trying for the new workers. In these circumstances feedback from the new employees themselves helped to sensitize the TAs.

Recommendations from Supervisors

A variety of useful suggestions for future programs emerged from the employment phase of the project. First, the transition to work from training is a critical time for all involved. Not only are the trainees adjusting to the world of work, but the supervisors and the TAs are adjusting to new working conditions as well. Consequently, an orientation program for all staff involved, in this case supervisors and TAs, is essential. It should provide information about the project not only in terms of the broader sense of its community objectives and contribution, but also in terms of the specifics that will affect the supervisors and the TAs. It should be emphasized that an understanding of the broader contribution being made by the project as a whole can lead to greater personal investment on the part of all the participants. This type of orientation can enrich employees' perception of their work as serving a broader function than their immediate job in a daily routine.

Second, the training program may not have adequately factored into its developmental curriculum sufficient specific organizational expectations that the women would face in the workplace. Since there was a desire on the part of all the actors that the women not be labeled or stigmatized, more attention to the final steps prior to graduation might have been less flexible and more realistic as part of the transition. For example, half-day sessions in the assigned work areas might have been useful.

Third, the staff should be more informed about the specific workers they will be supervising and receive more help in anticipating work-related needs and planning work. If flexibility is to be allowed in the work situation, this should be clarified at the outset.

Fourth, a buddy system should be put in place to provide both mentoring and modeling. The buddy would be an experienced worker. However, it was suggested that this not be just for the new cohort of employees but include all employees in order not to create the perception that the welfare women are special and different. The buddy system could be flexibly applied, allowing shorter or longer periods of mentoring as needed.

Finally, the supervisors felt a need for clearer information about the sources of support available to them and to the new workers both inside and outside the organization. The kinds of services available as well as methods of contact should be specified. Supervisors did talk to many sources including the employee relations department, Rickards, their own supervisory manager, and SETCO, but finding support usually depended on personal initiative. Instead, a systematic arrangement should be in place for use by all of the supervisors.

The shift from the transition period, post-training, to the regular ongoing work situation needs to be acknowledged and supported as well.

The supervisors made several interesting suggestions, none complex or costly, which should be viewed as more permanent, at least for the first year of the program.

First, there should be a structured weekly peer-group meeting of supervisory and technical staff for discussion of current policies and brainstorming solutions to specific problems. This would help supervisors work more comfortably and more effectively. It would also serve the organization as well because it would allow for a more consistent interpretation of company policy in regard to work standards.

Second, the support services available to supervisors and technical staff, either internally through the employee relations department or externally through SETCO, should be clarified on a regular a basis.

Third, training in communication skills would be helpful. Any different social group has different methods of communicating, both verbally and nonverbally, and training in the communication process would increase understanding and promote positive interpersonal relations.

Fourth, the importance of extra counseling and extra efforts on behalf of the new employees should be clearly communicated to the training assistants as well as the supervisors. The possibility of some informal bending of time and money expectations should also be in the picture.

Last, but not least, upper management should be brought in at the training level and the expectations for more clearcut support throughout the organization made evident at the outset. Related to this suggestion is the need for more reinforcement and recognition from upper management to supervisory staff on an ongoing basis to alleviate feelings of isolation and stress. It would have been helpful for the supervisors to know that their work was being acknowledged and was useful in the attainment of corporate goals.

Summary

An overall approach was recommended which highlighted the importance of integrating the new workers into the workforce as naturally and as quickly as possible. All strategies, including the buddy system, should be uniformally available to all workers. A second interesting recommendation was to use the new employees themselves as quickly as possible to help others, thus giving support and recognition to them as they succeeded in their new roles.

The workplace must also be seen as a flexible entity when a new program is introduced. This requires adaptation at all levels of the corporate structure. The native ability and motivation of the trainees is not enough to ensure success. There must be assistance from the corporation, as a partner in the venture, and this must be implemented through a flexible approach.

From the supervisors' perspective, it was essential for them to have an understanding of upper management's vision of the venture. This would have facilitated, and perhaps even ensured, a buy-in, a commitment, at all levels at an early stage in the process.

The supervisors agreed with upper management that the program was worthwhile, and justified the investment. While a few of the new employees did not stay, primarily because of daycare problems, and not the job itself, most of the graduates of the training program are still employed at Blue Shield and are very conscientious and career-oriented.

9

Perceptions of the Trainees as Corporate Employees

Pennsylvania Blue Shield speaks with pride of the performance record of the women who were hired from the Keystone training program. According to Tom Sommers, the overall performance of the program graduates was equal to or better than that of regular trainees at the six-month mark. Gerry Rickards noted that the graduates were productive as soon as they walked in the door, as opposed new employees hired in the standard manner, who needed ten or twelve weeks to become as productive. The relative performance for one Keystone class is shown in Figure 5.

This Pennsylvania Blue Shield venture offers a unique opportunity to examine the transition, not only from welfare to work but from training to work. Because this program was, in many ways, a first of its kind, all the wrinkles could certainly not have been ironed out ahead of time.

This chapter focuses on the perceptions of the new employees during their initial period of adjustment at the Blue Shield corporate facility. The transition from welfare to work raises a number of concerns and requires an array of new approaches appropriate for this critical period. Rather simple adjustments and structural arrangements made by the corporate employer can make a world of difference to the new employee.

It should be noted that, while the personal problems discussed in the chapter about the trainees are certainly still in the foreground of concern on the part of the program participants in their new employment

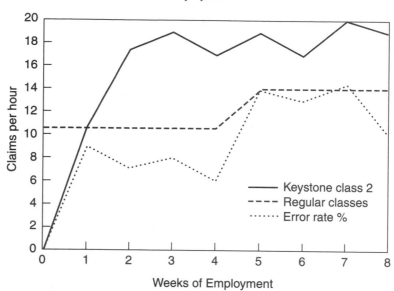

Figure 5. Performance of Keystone Trainees Compared to Other Trainees

status, this chapter addresses primarily those problems that are specifically work related.

Meeting the Employees' Needs

As is shown in Figure 5, the new employees made a successful transition into the workplace. In addition to performance, which is certainly an important measure of success, the concerns of the women themselves as they moved from the status of trainees to the status of employees are equally important in understanding this experience.

The transition from the Keystone training program into the Pennsylvania Blue Shield organization was not easy. In spite of the careful planning and preparation for the training program, comparatively little attention was paid to the beginning of the employment phase. This was undoubtedly due to the fact that the initial proposal for the program was aimed at obtaining funds to underwrite the training phase, which was something new for Pa/BS, while the employment phase was seen as a normal part of corporate operations. Therefore it was easy to overlook the detailed planning required at this next stage of the venture since it was now to be incorporated into existing organizational structures.

The women from the training program discussed some of the personal problems they experienced as they struggled to adapt to the workplace. According to Betty Johnson, the job counselor in the training program, this was a "rocky time" that had not been anticipated. Johnson explained that the women had graduated from the training program feeling competent and able to manage their lives. This new sense of empowerment had been fostered by the personal attention they received from the staff of the training program. In the workplace, however, the situation was dramatically different. The personal attention that had been the cornerstone of the training program was absent.

Pa/BS executive staff and the program's faculty had several major suggestions for smoothing the transition from training to employment, all concurring with the views expressed by the participants. All could be implemented by the corporation.

First, it would be very helpful to have mentors for all new employees in the early months of employment. These would be peers with whom the new employees could identify, and who would be there to help rather than to evaluate (as opposed to supervisors). In Johnson's view, such a buddy system would make sense for all new workers for the first few weeks and would not only make a big difference for the new employees, but would also have a positive effect on the entire organization by speeding up the integration period.

A second suggestion was to have a "point person" available to the group as a whole, someone the women knew from the training period whom they had come to trust, to interpret corporate culture, smooth over rough spots, and serve as an informal advocate and ombudsman for the new employees. An important aspect of this position is that the problems dealt with by this person would be kept confidential and not recorded in the employee's personnel file.

The point person could also provide continuity from the training experience with elements of the supportive culture the women had experienced, a point emphasized by Rickards, who commented:

> The environment that I tried to create was with hugs and also with a
> stick. The stick meaning that you've got to be able to conform to certain standards and when you needed a hug, somebody was there to
> hug and encourage you. When these young ladies come up and say,
> "Gerry, it was great," it makes it all worthwhile.

There is no question that gestures of warmth and informality made the participants feel comfortable in the training phase of the program. The fact that the work environment was formal and impersonal created a stressful situation which could have been mitigated by a point person.

Third, stigma was a real issue and created added tensions for the new employees who did not want their colleagues to know that they had been on welfare. Moving from one culture to another is always stressful, especially in situations where such stigma must be dealt with. Management was aware of the personal tensions experienced by the new employees, expecially in relation to the "we/they" stigma. Several women even resigned because of their feelings of insecurity. In a number of cases the staff reached out to these employees and persuaded them to return to the corporation. Corporations need to be sensitive to the issue of stigma and allow time for adaptation to take place.

Tensions were also created by the TAs, who provided hands-on supervision in the employment phase. The TAs had not been given an orientation to the program or any sensitivity training in regard to their own attitudes and prejudices in relation to both welfare and different socioeconomic and ethnic groups. Since they were often the key corporate representatives with whom the women were in contact, they occasionally seemed less than hospitable to the new employees. For example, one of the women reported that her TA made remarks that implied that she was different because she had been on welfare. Such episodes highlighted the need for the TAs to be trained in interpersonal skills.

Fourth, an extension of the probationary period would have been helpful as the Keystone graduates made the transition to the workplace since many loose ends needed to be tied up. From the vantage point of the new employees the corporation was not aware of their needs, and there seemed to be no give in the situation. Furthermore, the process of becoming professional requires time. For example, several of the women said that they realized that they had come into the workplace with an attitude problem that required adjustment. They had to learn how to interact with the other employees, especially how to handle frustration or criticism without becoming hostile or defensive. In other cases, they had to learn to make eye contact while communicating or realize that it was not professional to chew gum in the workplace.

The dress code came into play here as well. Dress was a major issue in the early weeks of employment. Blue Shield's expectation was that women would wear skirts and dresses to work. This expectation had to be modified since many of the women did not have such clothing. Instead, the only requirement was that they wear "clean clothes"—certainly a sign of corporate flexibility. The dress-code issue had not arisen during the training situation at Keystone, where the women did not have to be concerned with what they wore. The training program did focus on dress code with the emphasis on "present yourself well." It might have done well to realistically deal with dress code requirements as the women moved toward graduation.

In regard to the probationary period, Sommers indicated that the participants in the program were allowed six months to reach the required performance level, and in one case the period was extended to one year. This was in contrast to the probationary period of ninety days for regular employees. However, the women themselves were never aware of the company's flexibility in this regard. Informing the new workers about this flexibility would have encouraged them.

Fifth, another interesting suggestion, to rotate supervisors and TAs, was made by the participants to help in the transition. In being assigned one supervisor for the entire probationary period the new employee did not have the opportunity to experience different types of individuals or to obtain a broader perspective of different supervisory styles. Furthermore, when a personality problem arose between the worker and supervisor (or TA), there was no opportunity to try a different situation.

Sixth, flextime, which is a general issue for corporations dealing with working parents, would have been a real bonus for the Keystone group. Often the women were unable to pay for or arrange substitute care if a child was sick; thus their absenteeism was not a symptom of indifference, but rather a response to a lack of options for child care.

All the participants who were interviewed were clear about their commitment to their work and their eagerness to succeed and move up the ladder at work. They had goals which they sought to attain and were now more confident about their potential in the world of work. While they viewed Pennsylvania Blue Shield as a strict employer, as they learned to manage their time and money, the women felt they had grown in the process. Management recognized the fact that they were deeply commited to their jobs and had high expectations for their own performance. And yet, in spite of the personal commitment and goals, the extent of the ongoing need for on-the-job support had not been anticipated by either Pennsylvania Blue Shield or the other organizations involved. Many of the women had never held a job and needed tutoring in interpersonal relations, appropriate job conduct, personal finances, and other life skills. Some initial concessions were made by Pa/BS, but the support services offered were short-term, designed for the transition period only.

The final problem that the participants identified was an interorganizational one. The new employees were terminating their relationship with the Department of Public Welfare as they joined Pennsylvania Blue Shield. The transition, however, did not go smoothly. From the women's perspective, many of the caseworkers removed themselves from the picture, even though there were many threads that were not tied up. For example, many of the women did not understand what their entitlements to child care or health care would be during the transition period. One commented, "They cut me off welfare the day I started to work: no medical card for my children, no food stamps, nothing." In addition, there was often a gap between receipt of the last welfare check and receipt of the first paycheck; as much as two or three weeks elapsed before the first salary check was issued.

Job counselor Johnson was equally concerned with this issue and suggested that the corporation should have a fund available for the transition period. The stress of suddenly having no household income was horrendous for the new employees. (Johnson even gave some of them money on occasion to help them through the crisis.)

Summary

Moving from the world of welfare into the world of work is a complex process that requires careful nurturing. There are a number of concrete suggestions directly related to emloyee needs that stem from the Pennsylvania Blue Shield venture and which can be useful to future endeavors. Some suggestions are relatively easy to implement, others are more complex, but all should be carefully considered and seriously addressed as they reflect the perceptions of both the program participants and staff members. The following concerns are not ordered to reflect priority.

Underlying this entire discussion is the requisite of commitment and clarity regarding the mission and the goals of the program among all segments of the sponsoring corporation. There will undoubtedly be rough spots along the way related to the organization, the employees in the program, and the community in which it is lodged. The commitment will make it worth the challenge.

The careful coordination among the various organizations involved in the process is critical in the period of the transition from welfare to work. All too often much energy was devoted to the initial training phase, while little attention was paid to the employment phase. There is no reason why a delay in either welfare payments or paychecks cannot be prevented. Employees must be given a clear explanation of the transitional benefits to which they are entitled. Supplementary structures can be organized, such as emergency funds, to cover these eventualities.

Concern with the culture of the workplace and the company's readiness to accommodate a welfare-to-work population requires careful attention to ensure that all the players are ready for and receptive to this new reality. While much attention was paid to the preparation of the training staff in the Pennsylvania Blue Shield program, the lesson to be learned is that as much attention should have been provided to the supervisory and TA staff members directly involved in working with the new employees.

Perhaps the most feasible arrangement to be made is that of providing a mentor or "buddy," who would serve as a model to each of the new workers and be an important source of support in the early weeks of employment. The mentor could be either be a successful graduate of a similar program or a worker in the department who has the natural warmth and spark to be helpful to others.

Similarly, appointing a "point person" for the entire group could be easily implemented. This person, with whom a relationship of trust had been established during the training phase, would serve as ombudsman, advocate, and interpreter for the new employees. The point person would have the confidence of the workers because all communication would be confidential and would not be entered on the employees' personnel records.

A rotation of supervisors and TAs might be helpful to both the employees and the supervisors and TAs as it would allow for broader exposure to difference and would allow experience to facilitate the new and changing relationships.

The awareness of the need for warmth and informality should be stressed with the corporate players. Thus there would be some continuity from the training phase to the work phase. While the same culture cannot be duplicated, room can be made for more sensitive behavior and communications, a need often noted in organizational literature. At the same time it may be necessary for the training program to gradually move toward the more realistic culture experienced in the actual workplace.

Flextime is an issue for parents at all levels of work and in all work settings. Given the performance and attendance expectations of the workplace, the ability to make up time lost because of a family emergency would be a realistic arrangement. Pennsyvania Blue Shield demonstrated sensitivity to changing some of its requirements by relaxing the dress code. Flextime could take this sensitivity one step further and would facilitate successful adaptation by the employees to the expectations of the work environment.

If the transition from training to work is accompanied by an extended probation period, there is no question that a greater level of success would be achieved. And the benefit to society would be achieved as well as the move from welfare to work would be assured.

IV

TOWARD THE TWENTY-FIRST CENTURY

10

Where Do We Go From Here?

This final chapter, with its focus on future directions for both public and private sector leaders in the policy and corporate arenas, examines implications, raises questions, and makes suggestions that stem from the Pennsylvania Blue Shield experience. "Where do we go from here?" is indeed the question to be asked as the debate concerning welfare continues to unfold. This is also the question to be asked of corporate America concerning inclusion of social responsibility as part of its mission. This book has attempted to blend these public and private concerns focusing on welfare reform as a special arena for corporate involvement.

Much can be learned from the Pennsylvania Blue Shield experience vis a vis implications for public policy, welfare reform, and corporate social responsibility. The societal theme, however, has dimensions that reach even further than welfare issues. For those seeking a way to engage in the community but for whom a welfare-to-work program is not a possible avenue, a different example of corporate engagement is also presented. These issues are framed by the political and ideological changes that are occurring in the United States as we approach the twenty-first century.

Lessons from the Pennsylvania Blue Shield Program

Addressing a social problem as formidable as chronic dependence on welfare clearly requires the collaboration of the public and private sectors in our society. The lessons highlighted here are consequently directed at those in corporations as well as government.

The question of whether corporate America bears responsibility to address societal problems or whether Milton Friedman is correct in that making profits is the only social obligation of corporations was raised in Chapter 2. The outlook in this book accepts the idea that the well-being of corporations depends on the well-being of their communities. Recognizing that an optimal mix of bottom-line objectives with corporate responsibility is not easy to achieve, it is helpful to examine the conditions that make meeting these dual objectives possible. The readiness of executives and entrepreneurs to take the risk of producing such a synthesis reflects a broader view that recognizes the links between doing well and doing good. Since this corporate thrust is still relatively new, it becomes all the more important to examine the lessons from the few programs that have taken this path.

Many aspects of the Pennsylvania Blue Shield welfare-to-work program warrant attention and can contribute significantly both to the design of public policy and to the involvement of corporations in welfare reform.

First, the program was made possible through the collaboration of the private and public sectors. Without public funds for the training program, Pennsylvania Blue Shield would not have become involved, and without public-agency supports for the trainees during the program, the successful shift from welfare to work would not have been achieved.

Second, the operation was driven by the fact that jobs were reserved for successful graduates of the training program. This is in sharp contrast to most job-training projects for welfare clients, which provide training but leave the quest for a job in the hands of the applicant.

Third, a substantial number of welfare recipients were involved in the project. The program conducted by Pennsylvania Blue Shield trained 242 welfare recipients for skilled technical jobs the corporation had available and then hired 208 of these trainees into its workforce. The numerous benefits achieved by the program participants are well documented, as are the dramatic savings in tax dollars for our society.

Fourth, the project is unique in that training was recognized as the key to employment and it was carefully tailored to the specific jobs to be filled. Although the training program was nominally run by a separate subsidiary organization, Pennsylvania Blue Shield provided the content and instructors from its standard training program.

The Pennsylvania Blue Shield project benefited each of the various parties involved: the corporation, the welfare recipients, the taxpayers, and society at large. The following list summarizes the key features of the project, which can serve as guidelines for other corporate endeavors to address welfare as well as other societal problems.

- *Corporate self-interest* must guide the choice of activity; that is, a welfare-to-work program must meet a corporate need. For Pennsylvania Blue Shield, a new contract created the need for an expanded workforce that was well trained and stable. The project also served the interests of the corporation by improving community relations.

- *Corporate leadership and a commitment from the top* is a sine qua non for any societally oriented endeavor.

- A *long-term commitment* is important. It is helpful to develop a scenario that fits the corporate vision of a healthy community and outline the steps necessary to achieve it.

- A *supportive corporate culture* that is consistent with the corporation's particular social objectives must be shaped and developed. This includes educating the stockholders as well as the corporation's workforce at all levels.

- *Empowerment at the corporate level* gives the corporation control of the training and employment process. The corporation should set the criteria for participation in the program as well as performance standards.

- *Public- and private-sector collaborations* are essential for dealing with complex social problems. While public resources need not be relied on exclusively, they are critical in inducing the private sector to participate and in reducing risk to the corporation.

- *Federal and state programs* should be mutually supportive of local initiatives, especially at this time when more authority is being assumed by the state and local communities.

- *Multiple motivations* among the parties should be acknowledged. When diverse interests converge, there is a great opportunity for action to meet a broad array of societal needs and satisfy all stakeholders.

Since the link between work and welfare is supported by virtually all segments of the population in the United States, and work is viewed as the solution to the problem, it is important to identify the conditions necessary to achieve success in welfare-to-work programs. Again, specific lessons can be drawn from the Pennsylvania Blue Shield project.

- *The availability of permanent jobs* is a powerful motivator and incentive for welfare recipients who are eager to get off welfare.
- *Training* both in specific job skills and job readiness is essential for a successful transition from welfare to work.
- *Day care* is essential for workers with children. This need is best served by public programs until the welfare recipient finds a permanent position. American corporations should begin to consider day care a job benefit.
- *Other supports*, such as transportation and clothing, are essential. These can be supplied from any source but are most likely to come from the public sector.
- *Compassion and flexibility* will help to ensure the success of the target population, and are necessary to make the transition from welfare to work successful.

The United States is not alone among nations in dealing with the problems of poverty and unemployment. As discussed in Chapter 1, many Western nations are being challenged to develop new policies and programs in the context of modern technology and global economies and share the common goal of reducing expenditures. However, in the United States the solutions being implemented not only diminish the role of the federal government but even question its involvement. While decentralization allows states to tailor their welfare strategies through the mechanism of block grants, the protection and equalizing influence provided by the federal government are lost, as is recognition of the essential reality that we are one nation. The concept of a protective safety net for all citizens ultimately depends on the acceptance of a shared standard by all the states.

Current public-welfare policies in the United States do not fully take into account economic fluctuations, technological change, worker displacement, the globalization of production, or the downsizing of industry. And perhaps most importantly, they do not fully acknowledge the dominance of technological jobs, which require a sophisticated and trained workforce. The Pennsylvania Blue Shield program clearly responded to these realities. The experience gained from this program offers a good reference point for a serious examination of proposals to move people from welfare to work.

A Different Example of Corporate Involvement

A dramatically different example of corporate social responsibility is provided by the Tasty Baking Company, which is located in an inner-city neighborhood of Philadelphia. As early as 1968 Tasty became involved in a program for community development. The company's initial motivation was self-interest; the company wanted to prevent neighborhood deterioration, which would have a negative effect on its operations in the community where it had its plant. To work toward their goal the Tasty Baking Company founded the Allegheny West Project, which was originally focused on housing restoration and creative financing to help residents obtain mortgages. In 1974 the company founded an independent foundation, the Allegheny West Foundation, which became involved with a broader array of activities including social services, employment-related programs, and community organizing. The foundation is still active in 1997.

While self-interest was the original impetus for the founding of the Allegheny West Project, leaders at Tasty Baking Company were also deeply committed to community involvement. As was the case with Pennsylvania Blue Shield, both self-interest and social consciousness were the essential ingredients in getting started.

Also, as with Pennsylvania Blue Shield, a public program provided the incentive for Tasty's initiative, although it was not the only one. In this case, the Pennsylvania Neighborhood Assistance Act, enacted in 1967, was designed to stimulate corporate investment in poor communities by providing tax credits to participating corporations. The legislation ultimately provided a 70 percent tax credit against corporate net income taxes. However, only large corporations could take advantage of this tax incentive, since they had a big enough payroll to make the credit offset possible and worthwhile.

In 1993 Pennsylvania Governor Robert Casey and Philadelphia Mayor Edward Rendell, knowing of the twenty-five-year success of Allegheny West, asked Nelson G. Harris, the newly retired CEO of Tasty Baking Company, to head a community-development program at the neighborhood level in Philadelphia. Their interest in such a project was stimulated by a neighborhood-based program in Atlanta started by former President Jimmy Carter, which, upon examination, did not lend itself to replication in the Philadelphia context. Instead, the Allegheny West Project of Tasty Baking Company served as the model.

The new program, known as the Philadelphia Plan, was operated under the administrative supervision of the Chamber of Commerce. Harris took the lead in reaching out to other corporations with the objective of forming a coalition of corporations committed to community development. Personal contact at the top corporate level was the critical element; all thirteen corporations that were contacted became involved. Involvement meant a contribution of $250,000 yearly for a ten-year period, during which time each corporation formed a partnership with an inner-city neighborhood-based nonprofit development corporation.

The thirteen participating corporations include banks, insurance companies, utilities, and businesses (such as Allstate Insurance Company, CoreStates Bank, PECO Energy Company, and Tasty Baking Company). These are not local corporate entities; some are located in the suburbs and two are national in scope. All do business in Philadelphia and recognize that the well-being of that community contributes to the well-being of their organizations. While bottom-line interests motivate the participants, so does a sense of social responsibility, and the large coalition of partners makes a dramatic social program possible.

The 1994 mission statement of the Philadelphia Plan is comprehensive:

1. To substantially improve housing for the residents and provide for them both ownership and rental opportunities;
2. To raise the educational achievement levels of students, particularly in the elementary schools;
3. To enhance the capacities of neighborhood-based organizations and to work creatively with city and state agencies so that social and health services are available for all residents. . . ;
4. To refurbish public spaces and provide improved recreational opportunities for teen-aged young people;
5. To encourage and assist neighborhood-based economic development, particularly along the commercial districts, which will create jobs for area residents;
6. To create job training and referral services for adults and young people, including summer job programs for "in-school" youth;
7. To develop . . . educational programs for drug prevention and anti-violence initiatives;
8. To enhance volunteer recruitment . . . in the Greater Philadelphia area to support neighborhood coalitions so that every individual can become an active citizen.

The 1994 amendment to the Neighborhood Assistance Tax Credit Act served as grease for the wheels of the Philadelphia Plan. The Act is designed to

> encourage business firms in offering neighborhood assistance and providing job training, education, crime prevention and community services, to encourage contribution by business firms to neighborhood organizations which offer and provide such assistance and services and to promote qualified investments made by private companies to rehabilitate, expand or improve buildings or land which promote community economic development and which occur in portions of impoverished areas which have been designated as enterprise zones.

The legislation makes available a 70 percent tax credit to companies that make an up-front ten-year commitment of $250,000 per year to the community for comprehensive service allocation. The Neighborhood Assistance Tax Credit program is used to leverage the company's cash contributions. Although at this time only large corporations can be involved (due to the huge outlay involved), it is anticipated that innovative strategies will be developed to involve small and middle-sized businesses in the future. For example, five businesses can become entitled to the tax offset by combining their resources for the up-front contribution. Together they can then form a partnership with a designated neighborhood based nonprofit development corporation.

Like the Blue Shield welfare-to-work program, the neighborhood-assistance program is a product of public-private cooperation. The mission statement of the Philadelphia Plan concludes with the statement "This program represents an unique opportunity to bring substantially more public and private resources together in order to improve the quality of life for thousands of Philadelphia's inner-city residents." While this program is unique in meeting local needs, its elements can certainly be replicated elsewhere.

Summary

The lessons from the Pennsylvania Blue Shield can help those segments of corporate America which have an interest in contributing to the social good. They can also help legislators formulate public policy aimed at solving the problem of welfare through work.

The problem of welfare dependency is complex, perplexing, and challenging; overly simplistic solutions will not do. The fundamental question remains: What is our goal in solving this problem? Is it to cut welfare expenditures so that our taxes will be lower? Is it to create opportunities for individuals to lead productive and satisfying lives? Or is it to serve society as a whole by ensuring that certain groups in the population are not marginalized?

We hope that democratic discussion and compromise will lead to a solution that maximizes societal good as well as individual and corporate good. This case study suggests some paths we can take in meeting the challenge of welfare as we move into the twenty-first century.

Index

John D. Rockefeller, Jr. on, 19, 20
personal well-being from, 22
philosophy statements, 22, 33–34
profit margin and, 21–22
welfare reform strategies, 26–27
Cost-benefit analysis, 67–70
Creaming, 12–13, 38
entry-level trainee criteria and,
47–48
Creative Training Concepts, 37, 38,
39, 44, 51, 83
expenses, 68
performance-based contract, 49
staff preparation by, 57
on training staff selection, 55

Daycare. *See* Child care
Dress code. *See* Clothing

Earnings gains, 15
Economic conditions, 25–26, 112
Economic self-sufficiency, 9
EIPP. *See* Employment Incentive
Payment Program
Elizabethan Poor Law (1601), 7
Employment (Pa/BS). *See also*
Medicare claims processing;
Training program (Pa/BS)
absenteeism, 94, 103
buddy system proposal, 96, 101,
105
flextime proposal, 103, 106
hiring standards, 46, 49
job counselor's role, 60–62
job description and work expectations, 48–49
number of open jobs, 30–31, 40,
110
on-the-job support needs, 103–4
pay scale, 48
"point person" proposal, 101–2,
105
policy flexibility, 93, 94, 103, 106
probation period extension, 102,
103, 106
specific work issues, 90–91,
102–3, 105–6

supervisors, 91–97, 103, 105
technical assistants, 93, 95–96,
102, 103, 105
trainee graduation and, 82–84
trainee hiring and retention rate,
65–67
trainee integration, 87–98, 190–91
trainees' performance record,
99–106
training separated from, 36–37, 40,
44
and work ethic acculturation, 93
Employment Incentive Payment Program (EIPP), 50
Europe
Austria, work training programs, 8
child care facilities, 27
Glasgow (Scotland), training program, 9
Great Britain, training programs,
7, 9
training's centrality to social welfare measures, 7–9

Family Support Act of 1988, 9–10,
14–15
Federal government. *See* Public sec-
tor; *specific legislation*
Federal tax credits. *See* Tax credits;
specific programs
Federal welfare legislation. *See spe-
cific acts*
Federal work/training programs,
9–11
Female-headed families, 14
Fiscal year (FY) fixed funding, 6
Flextime, 103, 106
Friedman, Milton, 18, 110
"Friedman Doctrine—The Social Re-
sponsibility of Business Is to In-
crease Its Profits, The" (Fried-
man), 18

Global economy, 25, 112
Government. *See* Public sector
Grode, George, 31–32, 36, 77
Gueron, Judith, 15